T0219871

Communications in Computer and Information Science 732

Commenced Publication in 2007
Founding and Former Series Editors:
Alfredo Cuzzocrea, Xiaoyong Du, Orhun Kara, Ting Liu, Dominik Ślęzak,
and Xiaokang Yang

More information about this series at http://www.springer.com/series/7899

Peter R. Lewis · Christopher J. Headleand
Steve Battle · Panagiotis D. Ritsos (Eds.)

Artificial Life and Intelligent Agents

Second International Symposium, ALIA 2016
Birmingham, UK, June 14–15, 2016
Revised Selected Papers

 Springer

Editors
Peter R. Lewis
Aston Lab for Intelligent Collectives
  Engineering (ALICE)
Aston University
Birmingham
UK

Steve Battle
Department of Computer Science
  and Creative Technologies
University of the West of England
Bristol
UK

Christopher J. Headleand
Computer Science Department
Lincoln University
Lincoln
UK

Panagiotis D. Ritsos
School of Computer Science
Bangor University
Bangor
UK

ISSN 1865-0929   ISSN 1865-0937 (electronic)
Communications in Computer and Information Science
ISBN 978-3-319-90417-7   ISBN 978-3-319-90418-4 (eBook)
https://doi.org/10.1007/978-3-319-90418-4

Library of Congress Control Number: 2018941545

Printed on acid-free paper

This Springer imprint is published by the registered company Springer International Publishing AG part of Springer Nature
The registered company address is: Gewerbestrasse 11, 6330 Cham, Switzerland

Preface

This volume contains the post-proceedings of the the Second International Symposium on Artificial Life and Intelligent Agents (ALIA) held during June 14–15, 2016, at Aston University, Birmingham, UK. ALIA is a vibrant symposium bringing together artificial life and intelligent agents research, which have significant scope for cross-pollination of ideas and techniques.

The symposium comprised two keynotes, a programme of technical talks, a demo session, and a doctoral workshop. The opening keynote was given by José Halloy, Professor at the Laboratoire Interdisciplinaire des Energies de Demain, LIED UMR 8236 (Interdisciplinary Energy Research Lab) at Université Paris Diderot, on the topic of individual and collective behaviour in bio-hybrid systems made of animals and robots. This set the scene perfectly for the programme of technical talks on the first day, which were on the topics of robotics, evolutionary systems, and agent-based modelling. The day ended with a demo session. The second day opened with the doctoral workshop, at which a number of doctoral students presented their ongoing work to the audience, and received feedback from a panel of experienced researchers. Technical talks then resumed, on the topic of human-like behaviour. The symposium closed with a highly thought-provoking keynote by Alan Winfield, Professor of Electronic Engineering and Director of the Science Communication Unit at the University of the West of England (UWE), on the topic of ethical robots.

The review process for this post-proceedings volume was undertaken in three stages. The first round of submissions was for presentation at the main symposium. Submissions for the post-proceedings were then solicited from the talks at the symposium, and this gave the authors the opportunity to respond to the reviewers' comments and address any concerns raised during the presentation. A second round of reviews were then carried out, with a further opportunity to revise following these, before a final decision was made. From an initial 25 submissions, eight were finally accepted as full papers in the post-proceedings, with a further three short position papers and two demo papers also accepted for this book.

I would like to thank a number of people, without whom ALIA would not have been possible. The first thanks must go to all the authors, who responded so positively to the reviewers' comments in revising their work over the last 18 months. Indeed, thanks to all the participants, who engaged so positively and constructively throughout the two days' discussions. Sincere thanks must also go to the two keynote speakers, who set the scene for the symposium so well. A huge thank you goes also to the review committee, who are named elsewhere in this volume, and worked diligently and patiently in making recommendations on the submissions, and in helping to support the authors of the accepted papers to make their work the best it could be. For support and sponsorship, I would like to also thank the School of Engineering and Applied Science at Aston University, including specifically the two Executive Deans during the period, Professor Ian Nabney and Professor Bjorn Birgisson. Their support enabled us to ensure that the symposium remained affordable and this played a large role in encouraging substantial student participation. Most of all, I would like to thank my co-organisers and co-editors: to Steve Battle, for coordinating the demo session and papers, to Panagiotis Ritsos for organising and chairing the doctoral workshop, and and finally to Chris Headleand for conceiving and establishing the ALIA symposium series, and also for providing the guidance needed to help make this edition the success that it was.

December 2017   Peter R. Lewis

Organisation

ALIA 2016 was hosted by Aston University, and was organised by the ALIA Organising Committee.

Organising Committee

ALIA 2016 Chair

Peter R. Lewis   Aston University, UK

ALIA Founding Chair

Christopher J. Headleand   University of Lincoln, UK

Demo Session Chair

Steve Battle   University of the West of England, UK

Doctoral Workshop Chair

Panagiotis Ritsos   Bangor University, UK

Webmaster

James Jackson   Bangor University, UK

Review Committee

Llyr Ap Cenydd	Mark Hoogendoorn	Elio Tuci
Nelly Bencomo	Istvan Karsai	Karl Tuyls
Tibor Bosse	Johan Loeckx	Steve Phelps
Alastair Channon	The-Anh Han	Jeremy Pitt
Lukas Esterle	Leandro Minku	Simon Powers
Kyrre Glette	Emma Norling	Adam Stanton
Harry Goldingay	Tim Taylor	Franck Vidal
Benjamin Herd	William Teahan	Peter Whigham

Sponsoring Institution

School of Engineering and Applied Science, Aston University, UK

Contents

Human-Like Systems

Applications and Games

Modelling

A Schelling Model with Immigration Dynamics

Linda Urselmans[✉]

University of Essex, Colchester, UK
linda@lurselmans.me

Abstract. The Schelling model of segregation since its first appearance in 1969 has enjoyed widespread popularity for its ability to generate patterns of segregation akin to those found in the many cities over the world to this day. This paper builds on this model to evaluate the effects of migration on segregation levels and segregating behaviour. In the wake of current political events such as the large-scale influx of refugees into Europe, I investigate how the scale of migration impacts the ethnic makeup of existing populations and how the overall satisfaction is affected. The results show that size and scale can impact a population differently, but that the crucial explanatory factor is the population density.

The Schelling model in its current form was published in 1971 by Thomas Schelling in a bid to understand how individual decisions of agents to relocate could lead to a macro pattern of segregation [10]. In the context of widespread racial segregation in the US, the model could demonstrate that for segregation to occur on a macro scale, no deeply entrenched racism was required- even slight preferences to reside with people of ones' own colour could lead to segregated areas. The model has since been adapted and advanced in multiple ways and is a well-known model of self-sorting behaviour. A recent adaptation by Hatna and Benenson [6] incorporates assumptions of a heterogeneous society in which preferences for friendly neighbours would vary. This paper builds on their model and tests in how far the rules can simulate patterns of migration in segregated cities. The literature on migration has not featured a Schelling model implementing external migration onto the existing grid (rather, already existing agents migrate within the grid). Contrary to usual models of migration, this paper does not offer an explanation as to why immigration occurs; this is treated as a given. Rather, the size, rate and composition of migration are the crucial variables that are under investigation.

The migration literature has enjoyed a host of agent-based approaches (see [7] for an overview), but mostly in order to explain why migration occurs. In the scenarios that this paper considers, migration is taken as a given, but its intensity (how often does it occur, and how many migrants arrive) and the makeup of incoming migrants differs. The goal of this paper is two-fold. Firstly, it seeks to add to the theoretical insights that the Schelling model can give us, not just for

P. R. Lewis et al. (Eds.): ALIA 2016, CCIS 732, pp. 3–15, 2018.
https://doi.org/10.1007/978-3-319-90418-4_1

migration but for general behaviour under conditions of sudden external shocks. Secondly, it seeks to evaluate whether and how the group of newly arriving agents affect the future pattern of the population. In order to simplify replicating experiments, the model is based on the aforementioned Hatna and Benenson study. Based on their description of the model details, I recreate their model and then proceed to adapt the model in order to test for my hypothesis.

The structure of this paper is as follows. The first part briefly summarises previous research done in the areas of migration and ethnic segregation, and lastly how Schelling models in general operate. The following paragraphs discuss how Schelling and migration can be combined, and how the model implements the migration element. Afterwards, the data collection is discussed and the results are presented through analysis and a brief discussion follows at the end.

Migration and ethnic segregation in the existing literature. The combination of migration and ethnic (residential) segregation has an intuitive appeal. Immigrants tend to cluster spatially [3], and so do ethnic groups [12]. Migration is usually defined as the movement of people from one place to another. These can be countries, regions, boroughs, cities or neighbourhoods. The type of migration that is of interest to this paper is international migration of people from their country of origin to another country (host country). When migrants enter a country, their point of entry is not random. Cities such as London have distinct areas that are well-known for accommodating newly arrived migrants [5]. International migration is still increasing [1] and affects the ethnic makeup of global cities such as New York or London. Ethnic segregation, occurs when people perceive a group of other people as different based on ethnicity and subsequently seek to live in closer proximity to people more like themselves. Migrants are an obvious group that can be singled out as 'different' since they are foreign to the country. This can, but must not, be linked to differences in ethnicity. Visually poignant features such as skin colour make it easy for people to distinguish between those alike and those that are different. Studies on migration and ethnic diversity are widespread. Putnam [9] finds that migration can increase the social costs of cooperation if the resulting society is more diverse. The proposed link between high diversity and low social capital has since been tested, yielding contradictory results, most likely due to differences in operationalisation of the social variables (see [2] for more discussion) (Fig. 1).

Migration is likely to make a difference to patterns of segregation. In a separate literature that is primarily concerned with international migration, a subject of interest oftentimes are diasporas: pre-existing communities of foreigners that exert a form of attraction to fellow countrymen and women to move to the diaspora [4]. Diasporas thus grow larger and faster after forming, until a point is reached at which the host population grows weary of its size and spread, and political measures are employed to reduce the growth of diasporas. Diaspora growth has been linked to the gravity model of migration: migrants are pulled towards already existing migrants, even in the absence of pre-existing family ties [7].

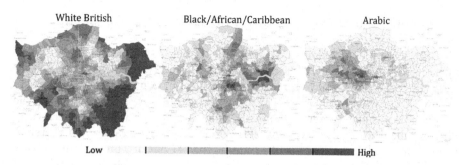

Fig. 1. The ethnic makeup of London in percentages, based on 2011 Census Data.

It is thus an intuitive conclusion that the rate of flow of migrants is at least in part a function of the existing "map": what country they move to and how the ethnic make-up of a country is shaped. Countries without diasporas are less attractive to migrants [8]. Equally, the ethnic makeup of a country or city is (in part) a function of the rate and flow of incoming migrants.

1 The Schelling Model

The basic idea of the Schelling model is that there exist two groups of people (usually represented through different colours) in a two-dimensional world (in this case a torus, i.e. there are no edges). In every group, the people (agents) have different preferences as to how many friends they tolerate in their vicinity. Friends are people of their own colour. In Schelling's original model, all agents share the same preference. The preference f (friend) is the fraction of like-coloured agents that is preferred. The model shows critical thresholds at $f = 0.3$ and $f = 0.7$, the former leading to a complete dispersal of greens and blues, the latter leading to distinct groups of segregated agents. Schelling's model showed that people do not need to be extremist in order to live in segregated neighbourhoods- in fact, even when people prefer mixed neighbourhoods, the aggregate pattern still tends towards segregation. For example, a person that tolerates mixed neighbourhoods, but wishes to be part of the majority (i.e. $f = 0.5$), the aggregate pattern tends towards segregation: if everyone wants to be in the majority, it is not possible to live in a mixed neighbourhood and have people satisfied. Recent studies interviewing migrants confirm the preferences [12].

Hatna and Benenson [6] allow for agents to have different preferences, which is more realistic than Schelling's assumption that everyone has the same minimum threshold. They are able to show that with two preference groups, the setup can generate patterns of both integrated and segregated areas on the grid, which is in line with real-word census data of US cities 2010 that they cite: usually cities consist of both segregated and integrated areas [6].

2   Schelling and Migration: The Experimental Setup

The model is an adaptation of the Schelling model by Hatna and Benenson [6] with several additions. Agents can be of either blue or green colour, can be either happy or unhappy and have a preference for how big a fraction of friends (like-coloured) they want in their vicinity. If this preference is satisfied (i.e. at least the minimum is met), the agent is happy. Happiness gets re-evaluated at each turn. The neighbourhood consists of 24 tiles. Friend preference values can therefore range from 0 to 24. An F value of 17 means that 17 out of 24 neighbouring tiles should be of their own colour. This is roughly 71% of the neighbourhood.

All starting agents are green (the "natives"), all incoming agents are blue (the "migrants"). At the start, greens count 1250, and blues count 0. At the end, greens count 1250 and blues count 1200. Unhappy agents will try to move to a better location. They chose from a maximum of 30 empty available tiles and select one with a satisfying friend-ratio. Just as in the Hatna and Benenson study, agents will move to a tile with the same ratio, if no better one is available. Equally, agents have a 10^{-2} probability of moving even if they are happy. The intuition is that agents in the real world will also move due to reasons that do not relate to their neighbourhood preferences [6].

The following settings were applied, unless mentioned otherwise:

1. Agents have one colour; either green or blue.
2. Agents have one of two possible preferences: $F = 0$ or $F = 17$ (see Table 1).
3. The grid size is $50 \times 50 = 2500$ tiles.
4. The starting population density is 50%, and the final density is 98%.
5. When moving, agents consider 30 randomly-chosen empty tiles to move to.
6. The probability of relocating randomly (if happy) is $10 - 2$.
7. The model runs for 10^5 time steps.
8. Every treatment is repeated 30 times.

Table 1. Population at the end of each round.

	Green	Blue
$F1 = 0$	25%	24%
$F2 = 0$	25%	24%

Each round, every agents gets the chance to act upon their preferences. At first, an agent determines whether they are happy. It does so by collecting the information of their neighbourhood and evaluate whether their segregation preferences are matched. If not, the agent will move. In other words, unhappy agents will always seek to relocate, whereas happy agents will remain at their current location.

In order to make way for incoming migrants, the assumption that urban neighbourhoods operate at a near-full capacity (i.e. nearly 100% of the grid is

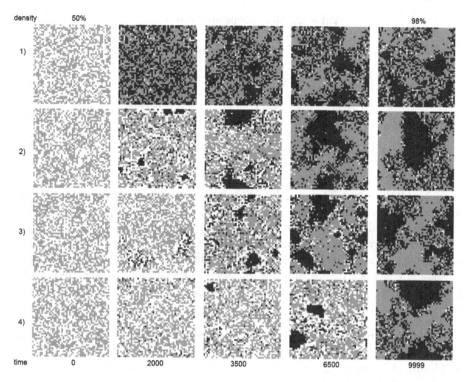

Fig. 2. The model over time (left to right). Each row represents one experiment. (1) influx of 1200 migrants once; (2) influx of 300 migrants four times; (3) influx of 80 migrants 50 times; (4) influx of 12 migrants 100 times.

covered with agents) needs to be relaxed. In the real world, cities can accommodate new citizens either by expanding in size (presuming that policy allows for expansion) or by creating new developments in already existing areas. In addition, current citizens can leave (due to various reasons). Lastly, the death of citizens can result in vacated properties. In this model, migration happens after a number of ticks depending on the experiment. The migrants will settle in densely populated areas[1], and then proceed to follow the same rule-set as the "native" agents (Fig. 2).

3   Discussion

Five experimental setups are compared. For every experiment, the influx size and rate is changed. See Table 2 for an overview. The control experiment does not contain migration and starts with a 98% board density and mixed agent groups. The influx experiment with a rate of 1 will insert 1200 migrants all at once, one time only. The experiment with influx rate of 100 inserts 12 migrants

---

[1] For a detailed description of the settlement mechanism, see the Appendix.

Table 2. All experiment parameters.

Treatment	Influx	Influx rate	Influx size
Control	No	n.a	n.a.
Treatment 1	Yes	1	1200 agents
Treatment 2	Yes	4	300 agents
Treatment 3	Yes	15	80 agents
Treatment 4	Yes	100	12 agents

at once, 100 times etc. The experiments compare migration happening at a large scale, as a shock to the existing population, as opposed to the piecemeal variant with very few migrants arriving but at a continuous rate.

In order to evaluate the impact that influxes of new agents have on the existing population and the differences between different sizes of incoming groups, the model collects data for multiple variables. The collection takes place every 10 ticks. Thus, a simulation of 10^5 has 10^4 data points. The variables collected are:

1. Global happiness: the number of all happy agents divided by the total number of agents.
2. Moran's I index of colour

The global happiness metric is collected to ease the comparison to many Schelling models that use the agent's happiness as the primary goal of the simulation. Oftentimes when all agents are happy, the simulation terminates (this is not the case for this model. The simulation will terminate after 10^5 ticks). It can demonstrate the upheaval that a new influx can cause. The Moran's Index of spatial auto-correlation is a measure of how clustered the agents are. High levels of Moran's I indicate high levels of segregation.

Figures 3 and 4 compare all treatments to the control. They visualise the different impact that each influx setting has. The one-off influx results in large shocks of happiness (dropping from 95% to 53% within one turn, see Fig. 3) and equally pushes both colour and friend-threshold segregation upwards. The control treatment has consistently higher values of both segregation and happiness, but towards the end, the values of both control and one-shock-treatment converge to very similar levels. The 4, 15 and 100 influx treatments show the same pattern: every time an influx occurs, the system experiences an overall shock relative to the size of the influx. The small and large step-like increases are very visible in the segregation patterns. However, as with the one-off treatment, all values eventually converge on very similar and oftentimes overlapping levels, showing no distinct difference over the long term. In other words, how often and how big migration happens does not change the circumstances in the long run. As soon as the density of 98% is approached, the model outcomes are virtually indistinguishable.

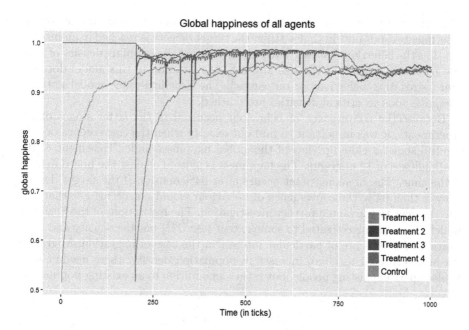

Fig. 3. The global happiness over time, comparing all four influx variations and the control

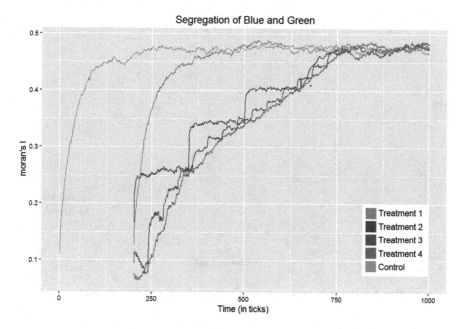

Fig. 4. The Moran's I of spatial auto-correlation over time, comparing all four influx variations and the control. Higher values indicate higher levels of segregation of green and blue agents. (Color figure online)

In the short term however, differences are big; in particular, the one-influx experiment stands out. In that setting, the target density is reached in an instant, and thus the behaviour converges to similar levels of the no-influx density of 98%. The results indicate that the size and rate of migration in this model does not alter segregating behaviour or outcomes[2]. The Schelling-esque model patterns emerge as soon as critical densities are reached.

Because the convergence of behaviour occurred in the latter stages of the experiments, it was important to find out exactly when the convergence occurs. Figure 5 shows a close-up view of the global happiness under Treatment 4, 100 small influxes of 12 migrants. The happiness is plotted against the board density at the time. The breaking point occurs after 94% density. If the target density is lower than 94%, the convergence of behaviour would not occur. For that reason, the density warranted further investigation. The restrictions of the Schelling model have been investigated to some extent (see [11]) but the density and composition of groups are of particular interest in the case of migration. Migration can be interpreted to be an increase in population density; there needn't be a displacement of existing people, but rather an addition to an existing population.

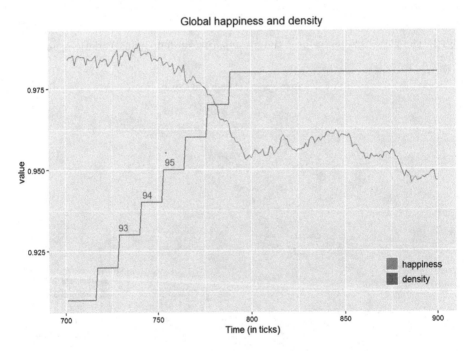

Fig. 5. Global happiness values between 91% and 98% density

---

[2] The same experiments were repeated using single F thresholds, as is standard for Schelling models. The convergence patterns remain.

4   Investigating Population Density and Ethnic Composition

To inspect the importance of density and composition, the model was revised: instead of migrants settling throughout the run, every migration is treated as a new initial condition. The amount of empty space that agents have in Schelling's model is significant: the more space there is for intolerant agents to "free" themselves from unsatisfactory neighbourhoods, the more likely they are able to avoid dissatisfaction. In general, more agents can be happy and much quicker in situations of empty space. Crowded places on the other hands introduce friction, as agents are not able to escape as quickly (if at all). Instead of focusing on the migration of blues and greens throughout, migrants are implemented at the start of the simulation as part of the initial setup (since it doesn't matter when they come in). In the previous model, both green and blue as well as $F1$ and $F2$ ratios were uniformly distributed, so that roughly half of the population was green (or blue), and half of each group would have $F = 0$ (or $F = 17$). These parameters are now altered.

What if the existing population consisted of both tolerant and intolerant agents, but all new agents are hardliners (or vice versa)? This could be reminiscent of a real situation in which there are groups of migrants that are culturally too distant to integrate; or equally, newly arriving migrants are met by a very hostile crowd not willing to engage with the new people. I test different ratios of green and blue and $F = 0$ and $F = 17$ under different densities to see whether they affect the long term outcomes. Table 3 summarises the treatments A-D.

Table 3. All experiment parameters of population density and composition

Treatment	Ratio Green-Blue	Ratio Green F1/F2	Ratio Blue F1/F2	Density
Treatment A	50% – 50%	50% – 50%	50% – 50%	88%, 96%
Treatment B	70% – 30%	50% – 50%	50% – 50%	88%, 96%
Treatment C	50% – 50%	90% – 10%	10% – 90%	88%, 96%
Treatment D	50% – 50%	90% – 10%	90% – 10%	88%, 96%

Treatment A uses the same even split that was employed in the earlier stages of the analysis; treatment B retains the even split of moderates and hardliners, but features a larger native population (70% of all agents). Treatment C has an evenly split native-migrant population, but of all the natives, only 10% are hardliners whereas among the migrants, 90% are. The final treatment differs from C only in that migrants feature few hardliners just as the natives do, with 10%. Every treatment is repeated under conditions of 88% and 96% density. The densities were chosen because they lie below and above the critical threshold of convergent behaviour, respectively (see Fig. 5). Both global happiness and the Moran's I are collected again.

The results for this experiment are shown in Figs. 6 and 7.

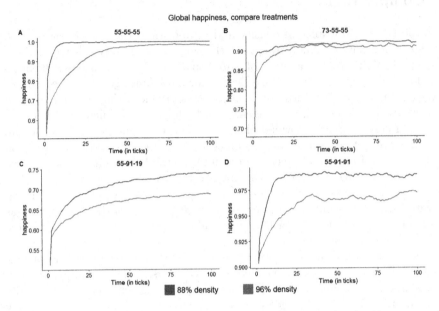

Fig. 6. The global happiness comparing 88% and 96% density levels. Treatments A, B, C and D (see Table 3)

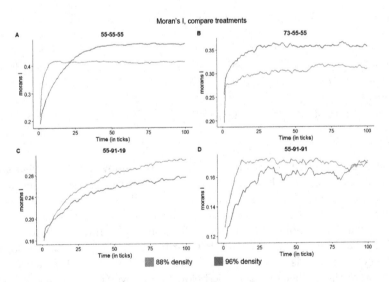

Fig. 7. The Moran's I of spatial auto-correlation, comparing 88% and 96% density levels. Treatments A, B, C and D (see Table 3)

As a general rule, the global happiness values show the same converging pattern, although under conditions of higher density, it takes longer to reach these values. In treatment A, for a global happiness of at least 97% to be reached, agents in a densely populated environment need 70 time steps- the same agents on 88% board density need a mere 20 time steps and retain their high happiness throughout. Overall, lower density results in higher happiness levels compared to the higher density setup. However, there are distinct trends of note: the relative difference is higher (and significant) in treatments C and D. Density becomes an important driver of happiness if the F-values are not evenly split. The C treatment, unique in its setup of 90% hardliner migrants, has the lowest levels of absolute happiness, never reaching 75% overall, even under conditions of lower density. This is intuitive given that much more hardliner preferences have to be accommodated, and they are unlikely to settle happily.

The segregation between blue and green agents (Moran's I) follows a different pattern. Conditions of higher density result in higher levels of segregation, but only if the number of tolerant agents and hardliners is evenly split (A and B). Intuitively, with fewer migrants than natives (B), overall segregation levels are lower. The size and occurrence of clusters is not as big, and thus, the Moran's I peaks at around 35% segregation compared to 47% in treatment A. Treatment C and D have large tolerant native populations, resulting in much less segregation. Having 90% migrant hardliners (C) drives segregation up, but not above 30%. It seems that the hardliners are well-compensated by the large tolerant crowd. The trend is further downwards when almost all agents are tolerant (D). What is interesting here is that both C and D treatments, the effect of density is reversed. Higher density leads to lower levels of segregation (although this pattern is only robust in the C treatment). This is intuitive given that less dense populations offer more room to escape, encouraging clustering through freedom of movement. Although hardliners are more unhappy in dense settings, they also have less room to maneuver and are less likely to find a sufficiently segregated neighbourhood.

The two sets of graphs show that different composition of "migrants" and "natives" account for up to 5% of the variation in outcome, but the impact of varying the density is far greater.

To summarise, the density of the population amplifies segregation on both levels and impacts the happiness of agents in general. The composition of the population; how many are green or blue, tolerant or hardliners, is important but to a lesser extent. How well a population copes with a sudden influx of new people that are different along some cleavage (such as being a migrant) thus is largely a function of how crowded the place is in the first place. Short term differences between large and small migration flows can be explained by the variation in density that exists in the short term. More densities and composition combinations might shed more light on the tipping points which, according to the current state of this analysis, lie between 86% and 96% population density.

5 Conclusion

The results indicate that using a Schelling-model, the size and rate of migration of a new set of agents into an existing population have no long-term impact on segregation and happiness levels of agents. Any short term variation that may exist between large and small migration flows can be explained by the differences in population density. Further investigation of the model parameters showed that higher levels of density correspond to lower levels of happiness, but the segregation levels are more sensitive to the composition of agents.

When the number of arriving agents is low, agents have, on average, more empty space to use. Intolerant agents thus seek to belong to groups of their own colour, and if they are on the edge of a group, they are usually surrounded by empty space. Visually, this results in white buffer zones between groups. These zones do not appear if the population covers 98% of the map. Thus, agents on the fringe of a group will likely neighbour agents of a different colour, causing unhappiness and more movement. Because the space to move is so limited, constant friction keeps agents less happy and in a perpetuated state of seeking better places.

The research question of how the scale and size of migration affects segregating behaviour needs slight readjustment: scale and size of migration only matters under conditions of lower density, where overcrowding is less likely to cause constant friction. With more space available, differences in migrant and native population are more visible. It should be noted that the terminology of 'low' and 'high' density levels is relative. Whether a figure of 88% density translates into a highly or lowly populated population in the real world will shape any conclusions drawn.

The model shows that using the simple rules of Schelling, some conclusions can be drawn from migration setups- more crowded places will suffer more negative consequences of migration. I intend to conduct further analysis of the specific tipping points of population density and segregation behaviour.

References

1. UK Data Explorer Census 2011: Wards in London. http://ukdataexplorer.com/census/london/. Accessed 4 Jan 2016
2. Ariely, G.: Does diversity Erode social cohesion? Conceptual and methodological issues. Polit. Stud. **62**(3), 573–595 (2014)
3. Bushi, M.: Rethinking heterolocalism: the case of place-making among Albanian-Americans (2014)
4. Collier, P.: Exodus. Immigration and Multiculturalism in the 21st Century. Penguin Books, London (2014)
5. Hall, S.: Super-diverse street: a 'trans-ethnography' across migrant localities. Ethn. Racial Stud. **38**(1), 22–37 (2013)
6. Hatna, E., Benenson, I.: Combining segregation and integration: schelling model dynamics for heterogeneous population. J. Artif. Soc. Soc. Simul. (JASSS) **18**(4), 1–22 (2015)

7. Klabunde, A., Willekens, F.: Decision-making in agent-based models of migration: state of the art and challenges. Eur. J. Popul. **32**(1), 73–97 (2016)

8. Novotny, J., Hasman, J.: The emergence of regional immigrant concentrations in USA and Australia: a spatial relatedness approach. PLoS ONE **10**(5), e0126793 (2015)

9. Putnam, R.D.: E pluribus unum? Diversity and community in the twenty-first century. Scand. Polit. Stud. **30**(2), 137–174 (2007)

10. Schelling, T.C.: Dynamic models of segregation. J. Math. Sociol. **1**, 143–186 (1971)

11. Singh, A., Vainchtein, D., Weiss, H.: Schelling's segregation model: parameters, scaling, and aggregation. Demogr. Res. **21**, 341–366 (2009)

12. Søholt, S., Lynnebakke, B.: Do immigrants' preferences for neighbourhood qualities contribute to segregation? The case of Oslo. J. Ethn. Migr. Stud. **41**(14), 2314–2335 (2015)

Evolving Complete L-Systems: Using Genetic Algorithms for the Generation of Realistic Plants

Benjamin G. Fitch[✉], Patrick Parslow, and Karsten Ø. Lundqvist

School of Systems Engineering, University of Reading, Reading, England
ben.g.fitch@gmail.com,
{p.parslow,k.o.lundqvist}@reading.ac.uk

Abstract. This paper introduces the idea of producing a platform, from which to set into motion the evolution of a virtual plant. The plants are represented and generated using the mathematical formalism of Lindenmayer Systems, with the genome being embodied by the production rules and variables of the L-System, for both the plant and its roots. Evolution is then simulated using Genetic Algorithms, which are driven by a user defined fitness function, in the form of an equation. This is all packaged in a Graphical User Interface (GUI), allowing the user control over the different genetic operators of the genetic algorithm.

1 Introduction

Within the games industry, the creation of diverse and varying environments that display a high level of realism is an expensive process that takes many man hours, and is usually outsourced with commercially available asset libraries, resulting in many games looking remarkably familiar. This is maintained through every aspect of the game's environment; be it buildings, weapons, flora or fauna. One approach game developers are starting to utilise for the generation of unique assets in a bid to make their games more immersive and varied is evolutionary computation. Work has already been done to create buildings, environmentally impacted flora and dynamic weapons [1–3]. There is a lack of such a method for the generation of realistic flora.

This project represents and generates plants using Lindenmayer Systems (L-Systems): A parallel rewriting system, originally created by Lindenmayer [4] for the modelling of filamentous organisms, which were eventually realised for their ability to produce plant like structures. These are, in turn developed and progressed using the evolutionary computation technique of Genetic Algorithms (GA's). GA's are employed for their ability to solve problems that are difficult for people to gain a full understanding of, as well as generating unique and – on many occasions – unexpected results. By adopting GA's, the generation of the L-Systems will be analogous to nature, and will be free from the user's prejudice and their expectations of a plant.

P. R. Lewis et al. (Eds.): ALIA 2016, CCIS 732, pp. 16–23, 2018.
https://doi.org/10.1007/978-3-319-90418-4_2

1.1   Previous Work

Little work has been conducted in the field of evolutionarily generated plants. One of the first was Niklas [5], but in his work he used only three parameters to model the branching pattern, along with a very constrained evolutionary computation technique that relied on a nearest neighbour search among the parameter space. Jacobs [6] takes a different approach and makes use of 'Genetic L-System Programming', and in doing so proves that L-Systems are capable of being generated evolutionarily in the production of 3-Dimensional plants. However, Jacob's does so by restricting growth space to a set number of branches. This was a very different approach than the one taken by both Ochoa and Mock [7, 8], who used 2-Dimensional DOL-Systems (Deterministic and Context free), which is the simplest type of L-System. Despite this, they each used very different approaches in respect to the GA; Ochoa opted for a particularly advanced fitness function to try and replicate natural processes as closely as possible, whereas Mock utilised interactive selection, by picking and choosing the phenotypes he deemed best as the selection process. Due to the use of simple DOL-Systems, both approaches concluded that further work should be done in the area; with the employment of "more complex L-Systems, multiple production rules and 3D morphologies" [7, 8].

This paper presents initial work; demonstrating the design and implementation of a platform to solve a real problem in the games industry, as well as providing a new area of research in the field of advanced L-Systems and evolutionary computation that has been stated as missing in previous works with the furthering of evolution in multi-production ruled 3D plants that simultaneously model the root systems for a more nature driven approach.

2   Lindenmayer Systems

L-Systems are highly adaptable, and as a result have been used in varying applications, but their main areas of employment are in the modelling of plants and the creation of fractals. They work on the principal of rewriting the entirety of a starting string (known as the Axiom ω) simultaneously, as specified by a set productions rules. The simultaneous rewriting of the entire string by multiple production rules is what separates L-Systems from the better known formal grammar 'Chomsky Grammar'.

For example, given the axiom [ω: a] and the production rules [P_1: $a \rightarrow bb$; P_2: $b \rightarrow ab$], the starting point would simply be [a]. But, after a single derivation step it would become [bb], another step would make it [$abab$], and another [$bbabbbab$], and so on. This is a very basic example, the L-System used in this project makes use of a much larger alphabet, to facilitate the changing of angles and generation of polygons in a 3D space.

2.1   Complete L-Systems

This project uses one of the most advanced types of L-Systems known as a 'Complete L-System' for the generation of the plant, as introduced and formalised by Prezemyslaw and Lindenmayer [9]. This L-System is in turn made up of three levels: The 'Partial L-System' which captures the structural characteristics of the plant; the 'L-System Schemata' which defines the control mechanism for the resolution of nondeterminism; finally, the geometric traits are added, these give the values for the angles and growth rates. The Complete L-System is designed specifically for the modelling of herbaceous plants (non-woody), as they are predominantly controlled by internal signals. Due to this, they model the growth and development of shoots and flowers from buds.

2.2 DOL-Systems

For the generation of the plant's roots the simpler DOL-System was employed, due to the roots not requiring complex growth characteristics, as well as being hidden from the user in the virtual world so not requiring such a high level of detail. By also modelling the roots it provides a far more natural approach, especially with roots being the major determinant of a plants growth. But, as a result of using the basic DOL-System, root organs – such as tubers - are unable to be modelled; as a result of the simplicity of the L-System, though this leaves potential for future works.

2.3 Graphical Generation

Basic L-Systems are generally generated via 'Turtle Interpretation' [9], but with the project's use of Complete L-Systems an advanced implementation of turtle interpretation has to be utilised. The creation of such a system would be an entire project in itself, therefore an external program was used; cpfg [10], which is a plant simulator, and integrated into the program L-Studio. Cpfg generates a 3-Dimensional view of the L-System that allows the user to view the whole plant by panning around, zooming and rotating the generated structure.

2.4 L-System Evaluation

Not only does cpfg generate the plant to look at, it is also able to evaluate the L-System to produce outputs in the form of various files. These files are then taken and processed to gain empirical data on the plant, though some of the data requires quite heavy processing to gain the desired measures. The measures include: Number of leaves, number of flowers, bounding box of plant and root system (in all axis) and the surface area of a single leaf. Using this data, the GA is able to evaluate the plant to ascertain a measured fitness value.

3 Genetic Algorithms

The evolutionary component of the project is applied by use of a genetic algorithm. In this project, the genetic genome (the genotype) is made up of a set of chromosomes, with each chromosome representing some aspect of the L-System, with the resulting cpfg rendered plant being the phenotype. The GA works only on the level of the genome; as the genome is what maps to the observable manifestation that is the phenotype. The L-System is encoded into chromosomes by using the crux of the production rule, as the predecessor is always the same. For example, the production rule $[P_1: a \rightarrow bb]$ would be encoded to just $[bb]$ as the precursor will forever remain $[P_1: a \rightarrow]$; this is possible due to the framework employed that holds the basis of all L-Systems. The variables of the L-System are also encoded, but as integers, as that is all they are. Due to the project being aimed at user customisability, the GA is made as flexible as possible, and allows for a variety of different genetic operators to be selected and adjusted.

All aspects standard to a GA are set by the user, such as population size, number of offspring and number of generations. The other facets of the GA are also defined by the user, the intricacies of which are expanded upon over the rest of this section.

3.1 Selection

In the project's GA, for each generation there are two occurrences of selection; one for the selection of parents, and the other for selection of individuals to proceed to the next generation (survivor selection). To give the user as much control as possible, they are able to choose between two different selection methods at each stage.

The first selection method is just a random selection that provides no selective pressure (i.e. not an evolutionary algorithm). It merely chooses individuals at random, either for the selection of parents, or of survivors. The reason for having a method that offers absolutely no selective pressure, is to relieve some of the pressure of the GA to try and prevent the occurrence of a premature convergence on a local maximum.

The second method is a fitness proportionate selection (also known as Roulette wheel selection). This is where every individual is given a section of a "wheel", with the size of the section proportionate to their fitness. The "wheel" is then spun, and the nominated individual is chosen – much like that of a roulette wheel. The method ensures that individuals with a higher fitness are more likely to be chosen, but at the same time there is a possibility of an individual with a low fitness being chosen. This results in a selective pressure, while allowing for variation within the population.

3.2 Pool Management

The users are also given some choice in the management of the pools; after the parents have been selected and the offspring produced, the user can determine their fate using the variable 'jointPopSelection'. This is either set to true; in which case the offspring are placed back in the pool amongst the parents, or to false; meaning the all parents will be killed off and the offspring will continue forward.

This can have a considerable effect on the outcome of the GA, as it can be the origin of an extra element of elitism: Assuming the parents were selected using the roulette method and the pools were combined. This results in the children (of which some will be better than others) being among the parents (which will also contain better individuals than others), meaning the resulting pool could have twice the number of 'good' individuals, potentially resulting in elitism.

3.3   Recombination

Due to the disposition of the genotypes being primarily character strings of slightly varying syntactical nature, the recombination techniques have to be tailored specifically for each chromosome. This coupled with the rest of the GA being highly customisable lead to only one method being implemented for recombination.

The recombination technique employed for every string based chromosomes was a 'Cut and Splice' method. In this technique a single point is selected at random for each of the parent's chromosomes, the corresponding child's chromosome is then made up of one side of each of its parents that were split about the respective selected points. This technique results in varying lengths of genes; with a tendency to genome bloating with the passing of generations. This has caused occasional problems with L-Systems becoming so large cpfg is unable to generate them, in which case it is penalised by assigning the offending individual with a fitness of −1.

But, the variables chromosome is an integer string, and uses a different technique. Here, 'Uniform Crossover' is used: This technique uses a mixing ratio, where each of the parent's individual genes are given a 0.5 probability of contributing it to the child. Though it is arguably a poor method – due to its tendency to destroy any resemblance of its parents – however, it was chosen to prevent the continued preservation of the ends of chromosomes that is typical of crossover techniques.

3.4   Other Genetic Operators

Mutation

Mutation is used to conserve diversity within the population, and is controlled by a probability value set by the user. The value of which, is the probability for each member of the population to be mutated. An individual selected for mutation will then have one of the variables randomly reassigned another integer.

Age Death

The purpose of age death is to provide an extra dimension of realism, by not allowing an individual the chance to 'live' indefinitely, although it only applies if jointPopS-election is set to true. The user established value, sets the maximum number of generations possible for an individual to progress through. This can be used as a preventative to stop one especially fit member of the population from leading the pool to a premature convergence, and aids in maintaining diversity.

Injection

The injection operator is another aid in maintaining diversity within a population. The user sets the probability of an entirely new individual to be added in place of an extra child. This works in much the same way as mutation in the preservation of diversity, but is potentially less disturbing to the population due to there being no chance that it could cripple a high fitness individual.

3.5   Fitness Function

In order to provide flexibility over the solution and give the user total control, it was decided to employ a user-defined fitness function rather than a limited set of anchored functions. This was implemented by letting the users enter a mathematical equation as a string, which is then evaluated. It also allows for the static variables of the plant's attributes to be included in the equation by use of alphabetic characters (See Table 1).

Table 1. Fitness function alphabet

Alphabet	Meaning
L	Number of leaves
F	Number of flowers
w	Plant width
H	Plant height
S	Plant size (w * H)
A	Surface area of leaves
Rd	Root depth
Rs	Root spread
R	Root size (Rd * Rs)

This functionality was implemented using an external calculator library called Javaluator [11], that supports equations to be parsed in the form of a string, along with the static variables. From this the resulting fitness value is returned and stored alongside the genome.

The flexibility this provides is a key feature in the project, and grants the users a huge number of potential results.

4   Conclusion

The final plants generated by the system have produced a wide range of different structures. One example can be seen in Fig. 1, which was a run with the fitness evaluated as: R, where R is the encompassed area of the roots. What is interesting to note, although a complete coincidence, is a remarkable resemblance to the seed head and root of the common Dandelion (*Taraxacum*): This provides promise for the system as a whole in having generated plants of a familiar nature, and therefore can be viewed with confidence if evolving plants for an alien world.

Figure 1 is not the only example of a recognisable plant having been generated (see Fig. 2), with roughly 3% of the plants generated being identifiable to real plants to the author.

Fig. 1. Plant generated for [R]

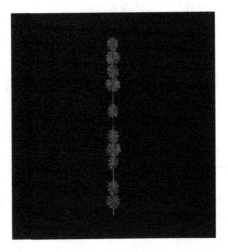

Fig. 2. Plant reminiscent of genus Leonotis

5 Future Work

The project so far – as initial work – has been successful, but is currently still a work in progress with many planned improvements. The main addition being the inclusion of other selection and cross-over methods, as well as additional evaluation criteria of the plants and roots, with the inclusion of tubers within the roots, – furthering the affinity with nature – coupled with a duel fitness function; allowing for easier driving of both the plant and roots within the GA.

References

1. Müller, P., Wonka, P., Haegler, S., Ulmer, A., Van Gool, L.: Procedural modeling of buildings. ACM Trans. Graph. (TOG) **25**, 614–623 (2006)
2. Shaker, N., Togelius, J., Nelson, M.J.: Procedural Content Generation in Games: A Textbook and an Overview of Current Research, Chap. 5 (2014)
3. Měch, R., Prusinkiewicz, P.: Visual models of plants interacting with their environment. In: Proceedings of the 23rd Annual Conference on Computer Graphics and Interactive Techniques, pp. 397–410. ACM (1996)
4. Lindenmayer, A.: Mathematical models for cellular interactions in development I. Filaments with one-sided inputs. J. Theor. Biol. **18**, 280–299 (1968)
5. Niklas, K.J.: Biophysical limitations on plant form and evolution. In: Gottlieb, L.D., Jain, S. K. (eds.) Plant Evolutionary Biology, pp. 185–220. Springer, Dordrechtc (1988). https://doi.org/10.1007/978-94-009-1207-6_8
6. Jacob, C.: Evolution programs evolved. In: Voigt, H.-M., Ebeling, W., Rechenberg, I., Schwefel, H.-P. (eds.) PPSN 1996. LNCS, vol. 1141, pp. 42–51. Springer, Heidelberg (1996). https://doi.org/10.1007/3-540-61723-X_968
7. Ochoa, G.: On genetic algorithms and Lindenmayer systems. In: Eiben, A.E., Bäck, T., Schoenauer, M., Schwefel, H.-P. (eds.) PPSN 1998. LNCS, vol. 1498, pp. 335–344. Springer, Heidelberg (1998). https://doi.org/10.1007/BFb0056876
8. Mock, K.J.: Wildwood: the evolution of L-system plants for virtual environments. In: The 1998 IEEE International Conference on Evolutionary Computation Proceedings, 1998. IEEE World Congress on Computational Intelligence, pp. 476–480. IEEE (1998)
9. Prezemyslaw, P., Lindenmayer, A.: The Algorithmic Beauty of Plants. Springer, New York (1996). https://doi.org/10.1007/978-1-4613-8476-2
10. Prusinkiewicz, P., Karwowski, R., Měch, R., Hanan, J.: L-Studio/cpfg: a software system for modeling plants. In: Nagl, M., Schürr, A., Münch, M. (eds.) AGTIVE 1999. LNCS, vol. 1779, pp. 457–464. Springer, Heidelberg (2000). https://doi.org/10.1007/3-540-45104-8_38
11. Astesana, J.-M.: Javaluator (2012)

Robotics

subCULTron - Cultural Development as a Tool in Underwater Robotics

Ronald Thenius[1]([✉]), Daniel Moser[1], Joshua Cherian Varughese[1],
Serge Kernbach[2], Igor Kuksin[2], Olga Kernbach[2], Elena Kuksina[2],
Nikola Mišković[3], Stjepan Bogdan[4], Tamara Petrović[4], Anja Babić[3],
Frédéric Boyer[5], Vincent Lebastard[5], Stéphane Bazeille[5],
Graziano William Ferrari[6], Elisa Donati[6], Riccardo Pelliccia[6],
Donato Romano[6], Godfried Jansen Van Vuuren[6], Cesare Stefanini[6],
Matteo Morgantin[7], Alexandre Campo[8], and Thomas Schmickl[1]

[1] Institute for Zoology, University of Graz, Graz, Austria
ronald.thenius@uni-graz.at
[2] Cybertronica Research, Research Center of Advanced Robotics and Environmental
Science, Melunerstr. 40, 70569 Stuttgart, Germany
[3] Laboratory for Underwater Systems and Technologies (LABUST),
Faculty of Electrical Engineering and Computing, University of Zagreb,
Unska 3, 10000 Zagreb, Croatia
[4] Laboratory for Robotics and Intelligent Control Systems (LARICS),
Faculty of Electrical Engineering and Computing, University of Zagreb,
Unska 3, 10000 Zagreb, Croatia
[5] IRCCyN - Ecole des Mines de Nantes, 4, rue Alfred Kastler, 44307 Nantes, France
[6] BioRobotics Institute, Scuola Superiore Sant'Anna, Pontedera, Italy
[7] CORILA, Consortium for Coordination of Research Activities Concerning
the Venice Lagoon System, S. Marco 2847, Venice, Italy
[8] Unit of Social Ecology, Université Libre de Bruxelles,
Campus Plaine, Boulevard du Triomphe, CP 231, 1050 Bruxelles, Belgium

Abstract. This paper presents the research done in the field of robotic cultural evolution in challenging real world environments. We hereby present these efforts, as part of project subCULTron, where we will create an artificial society of three cooperating sub-cultures of robotic agents operating in a challenging real-world habitat. We introduce the novel concept of "cultural learning", which will allow a swarm of agents to locally adapt to a complex environment and exchange the information about this adaptation with other subgroups of agents. Main task of the presented robotic system is autonomous environmental monitoring including self organised task allocation and organisation of swarm movement processes. One main focus of the project is on the development and implementation of bio-inspired controllers, as well as novel bio-inspired sensor systems, communication principles, energy harvesting and morphological designs. The main scientific objective is to enable and study the emergence of a collective long-term autonomous cognitive system in which information survives the operational lifetime of individuals, allowing cross-generation learning of the society by self-optimising.

1 Introduction

1.1 Concept

Underwater habitats are among the most challenging environments on earth: On one hand they are very interesting high-impact regions for the future of human society due to their richness in resources and their importance for climate and ecological balance. On the other hand, these habitats are restricted from exploration and exploitation due to their vast size, physical (current, pressure, turbidity) and chemical (corrosion, incrustation, fragmentation) conditions. There is also the aspect of minimizing the impact on the marine flora and fauna, since the ecological effects of past and present human activities in the worlds oceans have already started to show.

The aim is, to develop a swarm of autonomous robots to overcome the above mentioned challenges and allow the robots to operate in an out-of-the-lab, real world underwater habitat. This also includes interactions with humans doing their all day business at sea. We plan to solve the challenges emerging from this task by using bio-inspired concepts, as well in mechanical agent design (presented in Sect. 2), in algorithms design (presented in Chaps. 4 and 5) and in novel types of sensing and communication (presented in Sect. 2). In "classical" marine sciences, the monitoring of the environment is done by extensively equipped boats or single robots, that go to the point of interest and do a survey. This process is usually very cost and personnel intensive. We aim to develop a novel method for this field of science, that allows massive parallel measurements in a large area (e.g., for calibrating satellite pictures, observe algae blooms, migration of lifeforms), with a high data redundancy and comparatively low cost. The planned robot swarm will consist of three types of robots, that interact in a self-organised and decentralised manner, contributing to the over all swarm performance in different ways. We plan to enable the robot swarm to operate for several days or even weeks in the sea, without any maintenance, allowing to observe long time changes in the environment and development of behaviour in the swarm itself. The advantage of such an autonomous group of mobile measuring robots is that data can be collected in parallel in a large area. Further the robots can be programmed to react autonomously to a given situation, e.g., a high pollution value, and autonomously decide to investigate further, using autonomous task distribution methods [42]. The three robot classes created are described in the following paragraphs.

The aPad (Fig. 1) is a lily pad inspired robot, that will operate on the surface and act as a communication hub between the underwater swarm and the supervising scientists through both short range and long range communication equipment. It can dock and charge both aMussel and aFish and will act as a base station for these robots. It is mobile and is able to harvest energy through a solar panel. A detailed description of the aMussel can be found in Sect. 2.1.

The aMussel (Fig. 2) is a novel, mussel-inspired class of underwater robots. aMussels mostly reside firmly anchored on the seabed, having limited actuation but being able to resurface and dive autonomously. They are equipped with short range, directional communication, extensive sensing abilities and limited actuation. A detailed description of the aMussel can be found in Sect. 2.2.

The aFish (Fig. 3) are highly mobile underwater robots that will act as a transporter of information between the groups of aMussels and the aPads. Fish inspired collective swarming behaviour will be implemented to conduct exploration or searching scenarios. A detailed description of the aFish can be found in Sect. 2.3.

Fig. 1. Picture of the aPad in the Lagoon of Venice. The GSM antenna (top left), solar panel (central, black), four thrusters (submerged, orange colour) and the docking clamp (bottom left, submerged) are visible. (Color figure online)

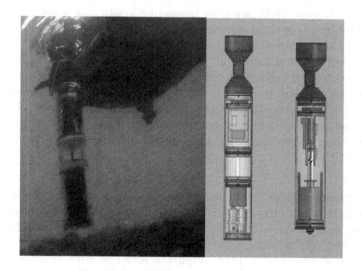

Fig. 2. Left: Photo of an aMussel being docked at an aPad, seen from underwater; The figure on the right shows cross sections of different buoyancy systems during design phase of the aMussel.

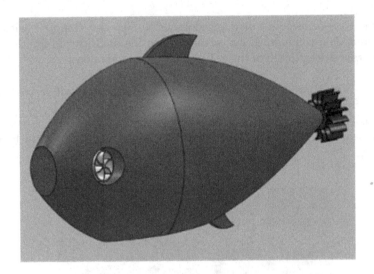

Fig. 3. Conceptual design of the aFish. The design is roughly based on the robot "Jeff" from the project CoCoRo [30].

1.2 Fields of Operation

The robot swarm is being developed to be used in two different complex and dynamic environments. Both are challenging from the point of view of robot and algorithm development and will enable a diverse swarm behaviour development. These two environments are described in the following sections.

Venice: The Lagoon of Venice is an interesting location as a test environment for swarm-robotics: the dense network of canals, the variability of the depth from 15 m to less than a meter, the variability of current and wind offer the chance to test the resilience and longterm functionality of a robotic swarm. Further the intense research going on in the Lagoon of Venice, be it regarding hydro-geology, or marine biology, allow to compare the delivered data to already done surveys, as well as to add the generated data to ongoing research projects [14]. Especially the dense spatio-temporal interplay of weather, sea, marine and coastline biology, humans working in the area make the Lagoon of Venice a challenging field of operation.

Mussel Farm: Another environment we consider suitable for our tests is a mussel farm, located in the north Adriatic Sea, two miles from the Venice coast-line. In this area scientists are investigating the interplay of marine life, marine industrial food production and recreational fishing tourism. One technique of observing these effects is to photograph the lifeforms with "photo-traps", or detect them by recording sounds they produce. A minimally invasive, long lasting approach to collect data (pictures, sound levels and prevalency etc.) gives the opportunity to understand the habits of these species without interfering in the on going processes. This knowledge can give insights into a more ecological management strategy in mussle farming and marine food production in general.

1.3 Robotic Cultures

One of the main novel concepts we want to investigate in subCULTron (as indicated by the letters "CULT" in the name) is the concept of "robotic cultures". Due to the high spatial and temporal dynamics of the test environments it might be necessary, that separate subgroups of robots have to locally adapt their behaviour. This can happen when a subswarm has either been intentionally dispatched to survey a local environmental parameter, or because of strong local currents or other dynamic influences of the environment that seperate parts of the swarm. The local adaptation can be generated by a swarm of robots by exchanging information about detected environmental features and resulting issues with used actuators, measurement systems or communication systems. This local adaptation can be easily transferred to other mobile robots.

1.4 Targets of subCULTron

We present a set of targets we aim for in the following subsections. The main objective is to understand biological, ecological, technical societies and their evolution. Additionally, the project also aims at enabling the socialisation of artificial beings.

Understanding Societies and Their Evolution: We address fundamental scientific questions about the emergence of large-scale and long term cognitive systems that go beyond classical engineering and computer science. Here, we plan to investigate the emergence of individual based behavioural patterns that form a distributed cognitive system by artificial evolution, life-long learning and learning-by-communication ("memetics") [10,13,21] based on evolved artificial neural networks ("proto-brains"). We plan to exploit fragmentation or clustering of slow-moving/stable agents that share/breed closely related behavioural traits as well as migration patterns of fast moving agents that carry traits across aggregations. We plan to investigate how simple, almost communication-less behaviour (less then 1bit/sec), as exhibited by simple organisms like slime mould, evolves into collective cognition. An algorithm developed in this direction is the FSTaxis algorithm [40] which is a bio-inspired emergent gradient taxis algorithm based on the behaviour of slime mould and fireflies.

Shaping a "Collective Being": We aim for a 3-layered architecture consisting of aPads, aMussels and aFish. While the aPads have global information, aMussels have access to only local knowledge and aFish are capable of moving in between agents with information (meso-local knowledge). We will investigate how those different types and levels of information quality integrate into one congruent system that achieves self-* and §-awareness capabilities ("*": awareness, regulation, organization, deployment; "§": self, group, culture, environment) over a long period of time (days/weeks). We will compare our agents' capabilities to eusocial animal's cognition by taking a socio-biological approach: How can cultural adaptation arise from altering group composition? We call this novel concept "swarm level programming" [16]. It auto-adapts the swarm not by altering the individual but the group composition as a whole. Consequently, an adaptive culture will emerge by adapting its composition from different sub-cultures.

The Minimum-Requirements of Communication: We will start with communication channels between artificially restricted (1bit/sec) agents, inspired by processes in nature, like slime mould [25], and investigate how minimum-requirement communication protocols evolve over time. We will study an "origin of language and signaling" by means of artificial evolution within our distributed robotic system. In fact, we plan to create self-adapting ecologies of interacting autonomous agents.

Establishing Long-Term Autonomy: Water motion is often considered a disturbance, but it is one that can be exploited to harvest energy or as "tool" for transportation. In order to achieve long-term survival of aMussels, we want to exploit underwater currents and residual organic materials for novel underwater energy harvesting [28]. In addition to that, aPads, positioned on the water surface, have the opportunity of exploiting solar energy to increase their runtime and exhibiting energy-efficient behaviors [2].

Development of Unconventional Communication Methods Underwater: Sonar is often used to perceive environment at large distances, however, it mostly performs poorly in short range. Performance of sonar is worsened in shallow waters charged with particles such as canals in Venice [27]. We will address this challenging issue by exploring the possibilities of a new sense for robotics named "electric sense" [6] that allows to perceive the world through the distortions of a self-generated electric field.

2   The subCULTron Swarm

To reach the above mentioned targets it is necessary to develop special robotic hardware, that allows to compose a swarm that is able to meet the requirements needed. In the following, the three robot types, aPad, aMussel and aFish are presented in detail.

2.1   An Artificial Lily Pad: The *aPad*

The final subCULTron swarm will include up to five autonomous floating and mobile robots inspired by lily pads in design (see Fig. 1). The concept of the aPad is to establish communication between the underwater swarm and the scientists observing and controlling the subCULTron swarm. They will transfer global information like GPS position, or mission critical information transmitted over GSM from scientists to aMussels through direct communication or indirect information transportation through aFish. For short-range above the surface communication wireless LAN and bluetooth will be implemented. The aPad will also be equipped with a long-range underwater acoustic communication device. The aFish will use the aPad as a base and charging station. There will be docking clamps to dock and charge four aFish at the same time. The energy necessary for this will be generated by a solar panel on the top, and stored in large batteries in the body. The same docking clamps used for the aFish can also be used to retrieve and charge aMussels that have resurfaced. The general design of the aPads is based on an autonomous surface vehicle for diver tracking, [23,24].

2.2   An Artificial Mussel: The *aMussel*

In contrast to the aPads on the surface, the aMussels will mostly sit stationary on the sea ground. Consisting of 100 to 120 units, this part of the subCULTron swarm will run in a constant low-energy consumption regime to allow extensive runtimes in the dimensions of several days to even weeks. In regards to autonomous robotics and especially autonomous underwater robotics these are extensive timespans. This will be made possible by energy harvesting from on board fuel cells and solar cells while on the surface. The aMussel will inhabit the sea ground in depths up to 15 m. Each aMussel is equipped with almost the same means of communication over and underwater as the aPad: wireless LAN, Bluetooth and acoustic communication which allows achieving consenus [20]. Another short-range underwater communication method called BlueLight that was developed in the CoCoRo project [22] and is based on high frequency light will be used by the aMussel. In addition, the novel and bio-inspired concept of "electric sense" (see Sect. 3.1) will be implemented to conquer the environmental challenges in navigation and communication that the highly structured environment of the Lagoon of Venice will present. The payload consists of a broad array of sensors that can measure current, depth, temperature, conductivity and turbidity of the water, a particle counter and a camera with lighting. To protect the sensitive payload of sensors and equipment from environmental factors like boats or heavy currents, the aMussel is able to open and close strong retractable shells. With it's retractable anchoring device and buoyancy control it is able to surface and dive autonomously. These mechanisms will also be used in novel algorithms for swarm movement without active actuators or motors, as seen in Sect. 5. The aMussel is a novel concept of an autonomous and cooperative underwater robotic cognitive network. In the project subCULTron, the aMussels function is passive and low energy, but still preserves the autonomy of each single unit and the resilience and functionality of the swarm as a whole.

2.3   An Artificial Fish: The *aFish*

The most actively mobile members of the subCULTron swarm will be the 20 to 25 aFish robots (see Fig. 3). Freely diving to depths up to 15 m, these robots will actively browse and forage the habitat employing fish-school inspired, self organizing swarm behaviours. As transporters of both, local and global knowledge, travelling between and communicating with both, aMussels and aPads, the aFish have characteristics of travelling salesmen in an underwater society. The aFish concept relies on the experience with the CoCoRo projects [22,30] "Jeff" platforms. subCULTron aFish are intended to operate in real-life scenarios, in open salt water. So, aFish are larger and extended versions of "Jeff", with greatly improved mechatronics in their buoyancy and navigation system. The added ability to dock to the aPad and environmental monitoring sensors (e.g., conductivity, temperature, pressure) make the aFish a powerful autonomous underwater robot with a runtime of one to two hours. The same wide range in communication from wireless LAN, Bluetooth and acoustics as the aPad is extended by "electric sense" and Bluelight for added underwater communication with the aMussel.

3   Hardware Methotologies

3.1   The Concept of Electric Sense

The Venetian lagoon and canals raises challenging issues (shallow, murky waters and confined spaces) to underwater robotics perception. To address these issues subCULTron will extensively use an original bio-inspired sense recently developed and named "electric sense" [5]. Electric sense has been evolved by several hundreds of fish species on the African and South American continent called "weak electric fish". To perceive its surroundings, an electric fish polarizes a region of its body (located in the tail) with respect to the rest of its body and so emits a (dipolar) electric field in its surroundings whose distortions by obstacles are measured by using several thousands of small transcutaneous electroreceptors distributed all over its skin. By measuring the difference between the currents with no obstacle nearby and those with obstacles, the electric fish can build a three dimensional image of their near surroundings (the range of active electric sense is about one fish body length). This sense is ideally suited to the conditions faced in subCULTron since it is insensitive to turbidity and works better as the space is more confined. Taking inspiration from these fish, in the context of the project ANGELS, a set of technologies (sensors), models and algorithms (control, perception) was developed, dedicated to this novel sense for underwater robotics [5]. The sensor consists of a set of metal electrodes arranged on the insulating boundaries of an underwater vehicle. Figure 4 shows a family of these sensors, named slender probes, as they are currently used to study electric sense [31].

Based on this simple design, one of the electrodes, named emitter (located at one end of the system), is connected to a voltage with respect to all the other

Fig. 4. Picture of a seven-electrode sensor organized in four polarizable rings, three of them being divided in two half rings allowing two lateral (left and right) current measurements.

electrodes (located at the other end) which are grounded and play the role of receivers since they measure the electric currents that flow in the underwater vehicle's surroundings after having been perturbed by the obstacles. Based on this technology that we named $U - I$, since we impose the voltage (U) and measure the currents (I), we recovered the range of the electric sense which is of about the length of the vehicle. Remarkably, with the same technology, we reproduced the passive electric sense which is a second sensorial modality of electric fish for which, the fish just measures an exogenous electric field produced by a conspecific or a predator. In subCULTron, we plan to implement these two modalities with the above mentioned technology. In particular, once equipped with this sensor and simple reactive control laws [6] (Fig. 5), each aFish will be

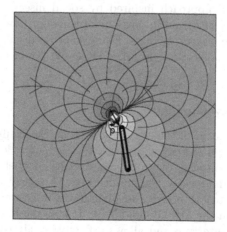

Fig. 5. The sensor tracks the electric field lines and crosses the iso-potential surfaces of increasing values.

able to navigate while avoiding obstacles (including other aFish) and to detect biologic materials (which are basically more conductive than water).

Electric sense will also be used to help the aFish to dock to the aPad by using passive electric sense and simple embodied control strategies. Allowing the aFish to follow the electric current lines which emanate from electrodes located at the docking station [7]. Currently we plan to equip our aMussels with electric sense. In this case, each aMussel will be able to emit an electric field in its surroundings (active electric sense) and to detect these of others (passive electric sense). Moreover, using several electrodes symmetrically arranged on their hull, electric sense will be able to infer the directionality of the received signals.

3.2   Energy Harvesting

The long runtime of the subCULTron swarm will be enabled by aMussels, which will harvest energy from their habitats and operate with low energy requirements. We plan to build on recent developments in microbial fuel cells [12,17,43] to take advantage of organic matter present in water. Bacteria naturally degrade the organic matters, and some species are known to be exoelectrogenic, that is, they can transfer electrons outside their cell to electron acceptors such as electrodes of an energy harvesting system. With careful regulation of the operating conditions, the microbial fuel cells will offer low-current output over extended periods of time. This allows regular environmental measurements and local communication with aFish. aMussels could also be capable of harvesting energy from water currents [35], complementing the output of fuel cells as needed. These natural energy sources will be diverse and will vary in the habitat in time and space. Hence, the robots will be the support of a micro-ecosystem. Our goal is to build an ecosystem acting as energy source for robots: We will identify its dynamics or patterns (oscillations, quorum), which can be suitable to store environmental information and at the same time enable sustainability. We will take a socio-biological approach inspired by social insects or marine colonial organisms, allowing us to establish novel algorithms for bio-inspired/bio-hybrid collective cognition in swarm robotics. Energy not used will be stored in standard LiPo-batteries, to overcome times of increased power consumption or low power production.

3.3   Electronic Development

Challenges in development of the electronic system, especially for the aMussels, are manifold. Long term autonomy of the aMussels require low power consumption, environment monitoring requires precise multi-channel measurements and socializing requires underwater communication. To satisfy these requirements the system is split into low-power and high-power subsystems. The low power subsystem is based on the MU3.0 module [9]. It uses the PSoC (Programmable System on Chip) architecture and allows a flexible easily customizable design. Ultra-low power capability allows running the ARM M3 core from 0.5 V with μW power consumption. The MU3.0 system uses a real-time operating system. The high-power subsystem includes a ready to use board (e.g., Raspberry PI) running a linux operating system which will be used for bio-inspired controllers and middle-ware.

In contrast to blue light communication modules in previous underwater robotics projects, project subCULTron will use acoustic long-range communication and n-channel electric sense for directional short-range communication.

One of the main challenges in electronic development is to improve the reliability of the complex mechatronic system. This consideration has been taken into account in the initial development phase right from schematics, PCB, component design, placement to wiring. The robots are planned as 'fully encapsulated', where the wireless recharging and wireless communication allows operating the robot without opening the body.

4 Evolution of Culture - Cultural Learning

The roadmap for the investigation of evolving robotic cultures and their applicability in swarm robotics starts from using simple bioinspired spatial structuring processes [39], simple movement paradigms [26, 32, 40], and task partitioning [37], and try to adapt them in an evolutionary manner, as can be seen for spatial structuring by [1, 36] or language [18]. The next step will be to use the processes found in basic human cultural development [4, 19] to improve the developed algorithms and methods, up to complex behaviours like e.g., markets [3, 11].

Another focus of subCULTron is the development and testing of the concept of "artificial cultural learning". As mentioned above the concept of "cultural learning" aims to solve the problem of a homogeneous swarm of agents in a dynamic heterogeneous environment: the members of the swarm have to adapt their behaviour (e.g., the way to measure the environmental parameters, the way of communication) to the local conditions. This can be done purely individual, or as suggested here, in subgroups. For a single member of the swarm it might be difficult to find a set of parameters for its controller, which is suitable for the given situation. If the sub swarm, that is in the same situation, shares the controller settings and the experienced impact on the functionality, it will allow to adapt as a subgroup to the local environmental situation. This process of exchanging, comparing and agreeing upon controller parameters (and therefore behavioural parameters) we call "local cultural adaptation". Please note, that this system will allow other members of the swarm that join the subgroup, to easily adapt to the given local conditions. Furthermore we plan to transfer well tested sets of controller parameters via mobile robots (aFish) to other subgroups. There the subgroup can test, if the controller settings transferred by a aFish are suitable for the given situation. In the long run, all of this leads to an permanent exchange of information between local adapted subgroups of robots. That will result in a swarm, that adapts to a spatial and temporal dynamic environment in a self-organised and decentralised manner. The development of such a system is one of the main targets of subCULTron.

Further we are (from a scientific point of view) interested in studying the relationship between the behavioural algorithms and their differentiations at different spatio-temporal scales (individuals/groups), especially in different environments (e.g., extremely structured areas, areas with periodic environmental events etc.). We expect to learn not only how to generate an adapted controller for the given task, but also about the influence of different types of environment features on different types of controllers. In the long run we hope to gather enough insights into the developmental processes shaping a robotic swarm controller, that we can investigate, if there are parallels between the controllers developed for our robot swarms and controllers developed by nature for real world swarms (e.g. honeybees, slime mould, fish-school). This comparison of the different outcomes of "swarm behaviour", "cultural evolution" and "cultural learning" will be done by comparing the evolved behaviours, as well as the evolved (or by learning adapted) controller structures.

In the habitats we plan to test our robotic system, individuals have limited perception and cognition, possibly facing contradictory short-term priorities. By testing the novel control paradigms mentioned above, we will investigate how different communities can cooperate and regulate their activities. Besides the already mentioned methods we plan therefore to use the concept of "swarm level programming" [16] to enable the robot swarm to solve the given tasks. "Swarm level programming" means to develop a group composition of fixed-programmed agents to "program" the collective behaviour in this way. Additionally, we plan use evolutionary computation to adapt this "role selection". This new approach can be interesting to answer questions from the field for natural sciences and engineering sciences in two ways: On the one hand, artificial evolution can find novel combinations of these algorithms that go beyond bio-mimicking and classical bio-inspiration. Thus, evolution will yield novel "beings". On the other hand, the intrinsic complexity and self-organizational capabilities of these algorithms can be seen as system-immanent "building blocks" that the evolutionary process is using. This way, algorithmic modularity will allow on-board on-line robot evolution [8,33]. We further plan to enable the robotic swarm to change it's configuration according to the environmental condition. This changes will be based on the measurements of the local performance of the swarm, done by each individual robot. The mechanisms we plan to use are inspired by the self-organising task allocation mechanisms of honeybees and other social insects [29].

5   Bio-inspired Controllers

The above mentioned concept of "cultural learning" (see Sect. 4) is closely interwoven with the concept of bio-inspired controllers. Besides the above mentioned processes of learning, we plan to use also predefined non-learning algorithms, that allow the robot swarm to generate something called "collective cognition" [15]. To reach this goal we plan to use algorithms derived from honeybees [34,41], ants, cockroaches, fish-schools and slime-mould [25] as well as from concepts found in neuro-endocrinology [36,38]. We further plan to explore the above mentioned concept of "swarm-level programming" [16] in the above described self adapting way, as well in a preprogrammed way.

Please note, that besides the more nature like "bio-inspired algorithms" we will also use more abstract versions of biological controllers, e.g., from the field of classical machine learning.

6   Conclusion

The main focus of the project lies on the development of a multi-layer robotic system that will use novel concepts like artificial cultural evolution and swarm-level programming to allow a self-maintaining robotic swarm to perform tasks in a highly dynamic environment. As test scenarios we chose very heterogeneous and dynamic environments: The Lagoon of Venice and a close by mussel-farm. These environments will challenge both, hardware- and software features of the robotic system that is being developed within this project.

Acknowledgments. This work was supported by the European Union, by funding the Project: EU H2020 FET-Proactive project 'subCULTron', no. 640967.

References

1. Auerbach, J., Bongard, J.: Dynamic resolution in the co-evolution of morphology and control. In: Artificial Life XII: Proceedings of the Twelfth International Conference on the Synthesis and Simulation of Living System, pp. 451–458 (2010)
2. Babić, A., Lončar, I., Mišković, N.: Energy-efficient environmentally adaptive consensus-based formation control with collision avoidance for multi-vehicle systems. In: Proceedings of 10th IFAC Conference on Control Applications in Marine Systems (2016)
3. Bowles, S., Gintis, H.: A Cooperative Species: Human Reciprocity and Its Evolution. Princeton University Press, Princeton (2011)
4. Boyd, R., Richerson, P.: The Origin and Evolution of Cultures. Oxford University Press, New York (2005)
5. Boyer, F., Gossiaux, P., Jawad, B., Lebastard, V., Porez, M.: Model for a sensor inspired by electric fish. IEEE Trans. Robot. **28**(2), 492–505 (2012)
6. Boyer, F., Lebastard, V., Chevallereau, C., Servagent, N.: Underwater reflex navigation in confined environment based on electric sense. IEEE Trans. Robot. **29**(4), 945–956 (2013)
7. Boyer, F., Lebastard, V., Chevallereau, C., Mintchev, S., Stefanini, C.: Underwater navigation based on passive electric sense: new perspectives for underwater docking. Int. J. Robot. Res. **34**(9), 1228–1250 (2015)
8. Bredeche, N., Haasdijk, E., Eiben, A.E.: On-line, on-board evolution of robot controllers. In: Collet, P., Monmarché, N., Legrand, P., Schoenauer, M., Lutton, E. (eds.) EA 2009. LNCS, vol. 5975, pp. 110–121. Springer, Heidelberg (2010). https://doi.org/10.1007/978-3-642-14156-0_10
9. Cybertronica Research, Research Center of Advanced Robotics and Environmental Science. http://cybertronica.de.com/projects/subCULTron
10. Dawkins, R.: The Selfish Gene. Oxford University Press, Oxford (2016)
11. Fleiß, J., Palan, S.: Of coordinators and dictators: a public goods experiment. Games **4**(4), 584–607 (2013)

12. Germán, B., Cervantes-Astorga, C.: Performance evaluation of a low-cost microbial fuel cell using municipal wastewater. Water Air Soil Pollut. **224**(3), 1–8 (2013)
13. Hougen, D., Carmer, J., Woehrer, M.: Memetic learning: a novel learning method for multi-robot systems. In: International Workshop on Multi-robot Systems (2003)
14. Institute of Marine Science, Venice, Italy. http://www.ismar.cnr.it/
15. Kernbach, S.: Handbook of Collective Robotics. Fundamentals and Challenges. CRC Press, Boca Raton (2013)
16. Kengyel, D., Hamann, H., Zahadat, P., Radspieler, G., Wotawa, F., Schmickl, T.: Potential of heterogeneity in collective behaviors: a case study on heterogeneous swarms. In: Chen, Q., Torroni, P., Villata, S., Hsu, J., Omicini, A. (eds.) PRIMA 2015. LNCS (LNAI), vol. 9387, pp. 201–217. Springer, Cham (2015). https://doi.org/10.1007/978-3-319-25524-8_13
17. Logan, B., Korneel, R.: Conversion of wastes into bioelectricity and chemicals by using microbial electrochemical technologies. Science **337**(6095), 686–690 (2012)
18. Marocco, D., Nolfi, S.: Origins of communication in evolving robots. In: International Conference on Simulation of Adaptive Behavior, pp. 789–803 (2006)
19. Martin, A.: Five rules for the evolution of cooperation. Science **314**(5805), 1560–1563 (2006)
20. Mazdin, P., Arbanas, B., Haus, T., Bogdan, S., Petrovic, T.: Trust consensus protocol for heterogeneous underwater robotic systems. In: Proceedings of 10th IFAC Conference on Control Applications in Marine Systems (2016)
21. Meuth, R., Lim, M., Ong, Y., Wunsch, D.: A proposition on memes and meta-memes in computing for higher-order learning. Memetic Comput. **1**(2), 85–100 (2009)
22. Mintchev, S., Donati, E., Marrazza, S., Stefanini, C.: Mechatronic design of a miniature underwater robot for swarm operations. In: IEEE International Conference on Robotics and Automation (ICRA), Hong Kong, pp. 2938–2943 (2014)
23. Mišković, N., Naj, D., Vasilijević, A., Vukić, Z.: Dynamic positioning of a diver tracking surface platform. In: Proceedings of the 19th World Congress of the International Federation of Automatic Control, International Federation of Automatic Control, pp. 4228–4233 (2014)
24. Mišković, N., Pascoal, A., Bibuli, M., Caccia, M., Neasham, J.A., Birk, A., Egi, M., Grammer, K., Marroni, A., Vasilijevic, A., Vukić, Z.: Overview of the FP7 project "CADDY - Cognitive Autonomous Diving Buddy". In: Proceedings of MTS/IEEE OCEANS 2015 Conference, pp. 1–5 (2015)
25. Nakagaki, T.: Smart behavior of true slime mold in a labyrinth. Res. Microbiol. **152**, 767–770 (2001)
26. Reynolds, C.: Flocks, herds and schools: a distributed behavioral model. ACM SIGGRAPH Comput. Graph. **21**(4), 25–34 (1987)
27. Proakis, J., Sozer, E., Rice, J., Stojanovic, M.: Shallow water acoustic networks. IEEE Commun. Mag. **39**(11), 114–119 (2001)
28. Rabaey, K., Verstraete, W.: Microbial fuel cells: novel biotechnology for energy generation. TRENDS Biotechnol. **23**(6), 291–298 (2005)
29. Schmickl, T., Crailsheim, K.: TaskSelSim: a model of the self-organization of the division of labour in honeybees. Math. Comput. Model. Dyn. Syst. **14**(2), 101–125 (2008)

30. Schmickl, T., Thenius, R., Möslinger, C., Timmis, J., Tyrrell, A., Read, M., Hilder, J., Halloy, J., Campo, A., Stefanini, C., Manfredi, L., Orofino, S., Kernbach, S., Dipper, T., Sutantyo, D.: CoCoRo - the self-aware underwater swarm. In: Fifth IEEE Conference on Self-adaptive and Self-organizing Systems Workshops (SASOW), Ann Arbor, MI, 3–7 October 2011, pp. 120–126 (2011). https://doi.org/10.1109/SASOW.2011.11

31. Servagent, N., Jawad, B., Bouvier, S., Boyer, F., Girin, A., Gomez, F., Lebastard, V., Stefanini, C., Gossiaux, P.-B.: Electrolocation sensors in conducting water bio-inspired by electric fish. IEEE Sensor J. **13**, 1865–1882 (2013)

32. Stradner, J., Hamann, H., Zahadat, P., Schmickl, T., Crailsheim, K.: On-line, on-board evolution of reaction-diffusion control for self-adaptation. Alife **13**, 597–598 (2012)

33. Stradner, J., Thenius, R., Zahadat, P., Hamann, H., Crailsheim, K., Schmickl, T.: Algorithmic requirements for swarm intelligence in differently coupled collective systems. Chaos Solitons Fractals **50**, 100–114 (2013)

34. Szopek, M., Schmickl, T., Thenius, R., Radspieler, G., Crailsheim, K.: Dynamics of collective decision making of honeybees in complex temperature fields. PLoS One **10**(8), e76250 (2013)

35. Taylor, G., Burns, J., Kammann, S., Powers, W., Welsh, T.: The energy harvesting Eel: a small subsurface ocean/river power generator. IEEE J. Oceanic Eng. **26**, 539–547 (2001)

36. Thenius, R., Bodi, M., Schmickl, T., Crailsheim, K.: Novel method of virtual embryogenesis for structuring Artificial Neural Network controllers. Math. Comput. Model. Dyn. Syst. **19**(4), 375–387 (2013)

37. Thenius, R., Schmickl, T., Crailsheim, K.: Economic optimisation in honeybees: adaptive behaviour of a superorganism. In: Nolfi, S., Baldassarre, G., Calabretta, R., Hallam, J.C.T., Marocco, D., Meyer, J.-A., Miglino, O., Parisi, D. (eds.) SAB 2006. LNCS (LNAI), vol. 4095, pp. 725–737. Springer, Heidelberg (2006). https://doi.org/10.1007/11840541_60

38. Thenius, R., Zahadat, P., Schmickl, T.: EMANN - a model of emotions in an artificial neural network. In: 12th European Conference on Artificial Life, pp. 830–837 (2013)

39. Turing, A.: The chemical basis of morphogenesis. Bull. Math. Biol. **52**(1–2), 153–197 (1990)

40. Varughese, J., Thenius, R., Wotawa, F., Schmickl, T.: FSTaxis algorithm: bio-inspired emergent gradient Taxis. In: Proceedings of the Artificial Life Conference, pp. 330–337 (2016)

41. Zahadat, P., Hahshold, S., Thenius, R., Crailsheim, K., Schmickl, T.: From honeybees to robots and back: division of labor based on partitioning social inhibition. Bioinspir. Biomim. **10**(6), 066005 (2015)

42. Zahadat, P., Schmickl, T., Crailsheim, K.: Social inhibition manages division of labour in artificial swarm systems. In: ECAL 2013, pp. 609–616 (2013)

43. Zhuwei, D., Haoran, L., Tingyue, G.: A state of the art review on microbial fuel cells: a promising technology for wastewater treatment and bioenergy. Biotechnol. Adv. **25**(5), 464–482 (2007)

A Modal Logic Analysis
of a Line-Following Robot

Steve Battle[1(✉)] and Matthew Thompson[2]

[1] Computer Science and Creative Technologies,
The University of the West of England, Bristol, UK
steve.battle@uwe.ac.uk
[2] Computer Science, University of Bath, Bath, UK
m.r.thompson@bath.ac.uk

Abstract. The behaviour of a reactive, line-following robot is analysed using modal logic. This provides an approach that is complementary to numerical simulation, allowing us to explore the qualitative state-space of the robot coupled with its environment. The envisionment of this state-space can be described as a Kripke model, and model-checking tools enable us to analyse this model to search for stable equilibria that contain goal states.

Keywords: Kripke model · Modal logic · Robotics

1 Introduction

Line following robots are extremely simple to build and are often the first kind of robot that a student of robotics will build. The simplest line-follower that can be built has a single sensor that provides a single bit of information indicating whether the robot is on or off a line. Similarly, we can set the motors in one of two states such that they steer the robot to the left or the right. Robots with such restricted input are often known as bit-bots [17]. In fact, this single bit input only provides the robot with information about one edge of a line. The best it can do is to weave along the edge, alternating between being on and off the dark area, with the edge between the two delineating a line as illustrated in Fig. 1.

Such a behaviour is easy to program, indeed a computer is barely needed, as the robot simply needs to react directly to the input. For teaching basic robotics we have been using the PiBot robot[1] programmed using Blockly, a visual programming language[2]. The PiBot uses differential steering where the left and right wheels can be controlled independently. If they run forwards at different speeds, the robot will steer to the left or the right. If the right wheel

---

[1] The PiBot is designed and manufactured by Harry Gee <http://www.pibot.org>.
[2] Blockly client-side JavaScript library for visual block programming editors. <https://en.wikipedia.org/wiki/Blockly>.

© Springer International Publishing AG, part of Springer Nature 2018
P. R. Lewis et al. (Eds.): ALIA 2016, CCIS 732, pp. 42–55, 2018.
https://doi.org/10.1007/978-3-319-90418-4_4

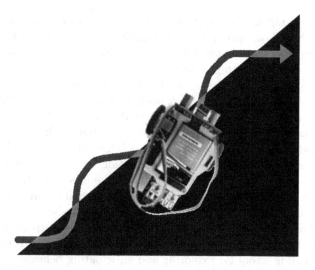

Fig. 1. Simple line-following strategy weaves along a line formed by the boundary between the white and dark areas.

runs faster then it veers left, whereas if the left wheel runs faster it veers right. The robot steers with the 'Set Motor left' and 'Set Motor right' blocks that can be set to a percentage of full-power. The 'Robot On Line' signal represents the sensor input from the PiBot's single, digital eye. In Blockly, a conditional 'if' block tests whether or not the robot is on or off the line and steers accordingly. To follow the edge, this process must be repeated indefinitely many times per second, so the condition is enclosed in a loop. The full Blockly code for this is shown in Fig. 2. It is fairly plain to see how this code works, and yet this account of the robot's behaviour is insufficient as it tells only half the story; leaving out the interaction of the code with its environment.

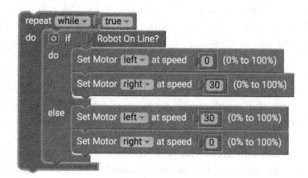

Fig. 2. Blockly code for the line-following robot.

For a more detailed and complete explanation we can, of course, create a simulation of the robot, specifically one that simulates the robot together with an environment. For the line-following robot we can specify a set of differential equations that define how the robot moves in a plane, and for a world without obstacles a simple image map serves to define the 1-bit sensor input. In a curious way this simulation gives us *too much* information. The way the line-following code works is largely independent of the actual motor speeds over a wide range of values. In the same way the mechanics of the robot, such as the axle length and sensor mounting relative to this, are also largely irrelevant and yet need to be specified exactly for the purposes of simulation. We're interested in how we build models to describe robot behaviour, that's the robot plus its environment, in an intuitive and qualitative way. To a first approximation *state machines* give us the tools we need, but again we want to emphasise that the aim is to model the robot behaviour rather than its software. The purpose of doing this is to support the process of understanding and designing how robots work *in the world*, providing a tool for exploring and anticipating behaviour. We are not therefore concerned with the problems of directly controlling a robot, with all the attendant problems of sensor and actuator noise.

The example of the line-following robot used here is deliberately simple, but it can be argued that most specialised robots exhibit only a handful of qualitatively distinct behaviours. For example, the iRobot Roomba® 400 series robot manual lists only 3 distinct cleaning behaviours ('spiraling', 'wall-following', 'room-crossing')[3]. Figure 3 focuses on the two primary behaviours of the Roomba robot, 'wall following' and 'room crossing'. When following a wall or piece of furniture the robot traces a curve that leads it to make contact, at which point it makes an obtuse angled turn and continues. Similarly, while crossing an open space, the robot eventually encounters an obstacle, where an acute angled turn will generally allow it to make another sweep back across the space. These actions cannot be carried out instantaneously in the real world, so they are modelled as state. The transitions labeled M are state-changes that the robot can influence directly; responding to the environment with a change in its own activity. Conversely, the transitions labeled E are caused by the robot's environment, typically an obstacle in the way of the robot. Thus we see two sub-cycles around 'wall following' and 'room crossing', following both M and E transitions.

Neither behaviour by itself provides adequate cleaning, but taken together they provide good coverage of open space and the edges. The 'room-crossing' behaviour is interrupted when it collides with an obstacle, at which point it may turn and cross the room again, or it may commence the 'wall-following' behaviour. The decision appears to be made endogenously. Then, to avoid the risk of getting trapped in a behavioural loop following the edge of an isolated piece of furniture, the exit from the 'wall-following' behaviour is again endogenous. For the cleaning robot to be effective it must have some means of switching

---

[3] iRobot Roomba® 400 Series Owner's Manual
<http://homesupport.irobot.com/app/answers/detail/a_id/843/~/irobot-owners-manuals-and-quick-start-guides>.

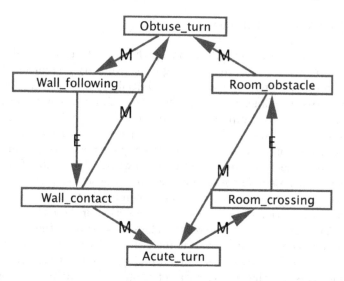

Fig. 3. This graph focuses on the two primary behaviours of the iRobot Roomba robot, 'wall following' and 'room crossing'. To ensure that the robot is cleaning the floor adequately, we would verify that it cannot become 'trapped' in one behaviour, but is able to switch between them.

between these different behaviours. These are the two additional M transitions from 'Wall contact' to 'Acute turn', and from 'Room obstacle' back to 'Obtuse turn'.

There is therefore no specific goal state, but we would need to verify that the robot cycles between these two behaviours. We *minimally* need to ensure that the transition graph contains a cycle that includes both 'wall-following' and 'room-crossing'. We will see later that we need to consider all possible environmental transitions E, as the environment must be treated as a capricious and potentially antagonistic opponent.

We explore the idea that modal logic is the most natural way to reason about this space of possibilities. Temporal modal logics already have a place in the formal verification of systems. Logics such as Linear Temporal Logic (LTL) allow us to reason about states that may *eventually* become true [11]. LTL and the more sophisticated Computational Tree Logic explore linear and branching models of time. However, circular models of time (as defined by a state machine) provide a simpler framework for thinking about repetitive behaviour and the search for stable cycles. In order to detect states that are visited infinitely often, an LTL formula may be mapped into a Büchi automaton [5]. However, the application of these techniques to open systems, including robots interacting with their environments, remains an open question precisely because of the adversarial nature of the relationship.

2   Qualitative Simulation

For a state-determined system [2], knowing the state at time t enables one to predict its state at time $t + 1$, representing some arbitrary increment. Any given setting of the robot's drive motors, and an initial orientation will carry it in a smooth arc across the plane. Taken together, the position, orientation, and motor speeds define a field of very possible trajectory. When we introduce the robot code the field changes and we begin to see trajectories that converge to stable equilibria [10]. We can think of a stable region as a cluster of neighbouring stable equilibria whose trajectories are forever trapped within that region. For the robot to be effective, such a stable region must at least intersect the set of goal states. The state-vector of the robot's environment comprises the coordinates on the plane and the orientation of the robot, and a function of these three values that determines the sensor input to the robot. The state-vector of the robot includes those values it has direct control over, namely the values of the two drive motors.

A central feature of *Qualitative Simulation* [8] is the identification of qualitatively distinct *episodes* that represent a set of states, and differ from each other in that they fall on different sides of a *limit-point* [4] such as being on or off the line. The process of enumerating all possible episodes is known as *envisionment* [6]. Given a finite state vector and corresponding limit-points, the envisionment itself will be finitely large. Qualitative simulation can be used in planning robot behaviour [16], where the performance of an action in a given state leads to a set of successor states, $(s_i, a_j) - > \{s_{i+1}\}$. The objective being to find a sequence of actions that transform the initial state, via a sequence of actions, to a desired goal state. Note that in qualitative simulation, these actions represent a change in the settings of the control variables of the system. These control variables are a subset of the variables that define the system and act continuously on that system.

However, this account gives an impression that the world may change only in response to the actions of the robot. Even in the simplistic world of the line-follower the goal state of being on the line is unstable as, unless it stops dead, the robot typically veers off the line. A corrective action brings the robot back to the goal state, the aim being to achieve a dynamic stability that passes through these goal states in a cyclic fashion. In other words, the line-following robot is an example of homeostatic control [1] whereby the robot takes corrective actions in order to regulate its position in relation to the line. In general, things may happen in the environment that are beyond the direct control of the robot, including the actions of other agents. This is the problem of *cycle detection* where the objective is to check whether or not a given condition can be satisfied repeatedly [15].

In our descriptive account we are primarily concerned with the robot being on or off the line. If the robot is off the line and turning right then it will eventually cross the edge, and conversely with the robot on the line turning left. However, if we place the robot further from the line then for a given turning circle the robot may miss the line entirely and will never reach its goal. Yet we do not need the detail of the exact coordinates or orientation of the robot. A qualitative account needs to work at a similar level of *granularity*.

The state of the line-following robot and environment may be classified using a number of logical propositions that define this qualitative state. The mutually exclusive propositions, *On* and *Off*, represent the single bit sensor and describe the qualitative state of the robot within the environment, being on of off the line. The state of the robot itself is represented by its heading, indicated by the mutually exclusive propositions *Left* and *Right*. If the robot strays too far from the line then its turning circle will no longer carry it back across the edge, and the robot is effectively *Lost*. This state variable is not directly observable by the robot. Together, these propositions define the combined state of the robot and its environment. The combinations of these domain values define a finite state-space.

If the robot's actions are held constant it is possible to observe the state changes that flow from starting the robot in any given position. Placing the robot in an initial state where it is on the line and turning left, $On \wedge Left$, we will see it cross the edge such that, $Off \wedge Left$. From there it may turn full circle counter-clockwise, re-crossing the edge. A physical robot will not follow a perfect circle and may well precess off into a region where it is effectively lost on a trajectory that no longer intersects the edge, $Lost \wedge Left \wedge (On \vee Off)$. With the robot heading left, the robot follows a similar, but counter-clockwise trajectory.

3 Modal Logic Analysis

Forbus adopted the notation of the temporal modal operator T to denote the time interval over which a predicate holds [3]. In this section we explore further the use of modal operators to define and analyse the behaviour of the line-following robot.

Modal logic has been used to formalize the behaviour of robotic systems; van Diggelen [14] uses a multi-modal logic to describe the range of actions open to the robot. Different actions represent different changes, which therefore cause different state-transitions. Our action logic is more directly inspired by Ashby [2] with all actions encoded as changes to state variables, the key difference being whether or not the robot can directly influence the variable (such as the motor speed), or only indirectly influence a so-called *environment* variable, such as the robot's position. This distinction between direct and indirect agency owes more to the work of Santos and Carmo [13] who develop a logic of action with these two distinct modal operators in the context of organisational theory. For example, a manager may have to delegate an action to an employee who has the skill to perform that action; the manager indirectly brings about the action that the employee performs directly. Similarly, our robot can directly change the speed of its motor outputs, but it can only indirectly change its position; a change mediated by its environment. We thus develop a logic with a modal operator M for direct motor actions, and E for indirect (environmental) actions.

This research was carried out using a tool called LoTREC [9] created by the Institut de Recherche en Informatique de Toulose (IRIT). LoTREC's primary function is the creation of tableaux proof procedures used to determine whether or not a given modal formula is *satisfiable*. In this application it is used to perform model-checking, to decide whether a specific formula is true in a given model. The model in question is a Kripke model, named after Paul Kripke who developed them as a way of thinking about *possible worlds* [7]. We can think of them simply as a graph with labeled nodes and edges that provide the semantic underpinning for a wide range of modal logics. Modal logic is often portrayed as an arcane field of logic with no practical application, but LoTREC invites us to consider modal logic as a practical programming technique, much as ProLog made first-order logic theorem provers a practical possibility for many applications.

The state-space, or envisionment, of the line-following robot can be enumerated by considering all valid combinations of the qualitative state-space propositions. Thus we consider the environmental input that indicates whether the robot is *On* or *Off* the line. At the same time we consider all the possible settings of the motor variables, turning the robot to the *Left* or *Right*. Like Forbus' T operator we label each possible world with the statements that are true during that episode (or state).

The next step is to consider the possible transitions between these states. As noted above, it is possible to hold the motor variables constant and observe the ensuing qualitative state changes as the system moves through its field. This could be done empirically, based on observations of the simulated robot. In this case the set of possible worlds is small enough that it is possible to enumerate them by hand and deduce the transitions through a number of simple thought experiments. In terms of the Kripke model, these transitions define *accessibility relations* between worlds. The state transitions we are interested in describe from moment to moment what might happen next, so they define a temporal *relation*.

3.1   Multi-modal Logic

We use the operator, E, to demarcate transitions that are driven by the environment. It is likely that there is more than one successor state in E for any given state. The transition taken really depends on many physical factors including the angle of the robot to the line, the curve and thickness of the line, and the current turning circle of the robot. In any case the robot has no control over this level of detail so we may as well treat this as a non-deterministic outcome. To avoid any confusion, for a state-determined system the next state is deterministic, however, once we aggregate sets of states into these qualitative episodes we may lump together different states that have qualitatively different outcomes. It is hoped that we may describe these qualitative episodes as 'states' without confusion, and with the understanding that aggregation leads to non-determinism.

It is unlikely that without any effective control that the robot could stay on the edge for an extended period. In this environment there are no naturally occurring equilibria that take in a goal (unless the robot didn't move at all). Motor actions allow the robot to directly influence a state variable; in this case the robot can change its heading by turning *Left* or *Right*. If we think of the environmental relation, E, as a set of railway tracks then this motor action is like changing tracks. It introduces a step-function that directs the flow of a field in a new direction, creating new stable equilibria where before there were none.

One may think of the behaviour of the robot pitted against that of the environment, as a two-player game. Each move is a state transition. The robot may allow the environment to make a sequence of moves until play reaches a critical juncture at which point the robot jumps in with an action that directs the flow of the system in its favour. In the case of the line-following robot, it waits for the transition in the environment that carries it over the edge of the line, and then switches direction that will later carry it back across the line in the opposite direction.

Motor actions, over which the robot has direct control, are represented by transitions labeled, M. For a simple *reactive* robot like the line-follower the model is only well-formed if it contains no M-cycles, as it should only react to external events in its environment, not to its own control actions, nor to a random variable. If it did then a cycle in the relation M might assume the appearance of a stable equilibrium (a sequence of control actions that return it to the goal) that is really masking an unstable equilibrium, like balancing a ball on the tip of a cone. The robot will inevitably cross the edge of the line sooner or later.

In a mono-modal logic the $\square$ and $\lozenge$ operators for necessity and possibility would be used. However, the multi-modal Kripke model used here contains two relations E & M, so we adopt the notation of subscripting the modal operator, $\square_E$ & $\lozenge_M$. Note that in the LoTREC output the relation is placed inside the modal operator using $[E]$ and $\langle M \rangle$.

LoTREC lets us perform a model-check on the envisionment, allowing us to confirm that it includes a stable region that intersects the goal. We define a proof-procedure that identifies a stable region. By querying a goal node with the statement to be checked we may therefore confirm the existence of a stable region that intersects that specific goal state. In other words, for the line-following robot we confirm the existence of a stable equilibrium that periodically intersects the edge.

3.2   Nominals

The proof procedure works by asserting a statement to be checked at the goal node and then recursively exploring the graph of successor states until it loops back to the goal node. If there is no such loop then the node does not appear within a stable equilibrium. This recursive search must therefore include a way to recognise the target node at which the search was initiated. Prior's *hybrid tense logic* [12] extends modal logic by defining a way to talk about specific moments in time such as 'now'. Should two possible worlds arise with the same name, it is guaranteed that they are identical (there is only one 'now'). Hybrid logic introduces the *nominal* operator, written '@', which enables us to talk about the target state, identified simply as @$_{goal}$. As the search fans out through the state-space, we can be sure that if we encounter another node with the same name then we have discovered a cycle that brings us back to the original state. The proof-procedure therefore terminates when the successor state is labeled by @$_{goal}$.

Given a goal node identified by the nominal $@_{goal}$, the assertion we want to check against the model is that there is a stable equilibrium that returns it to *goal*. Not only must there be at least one cycle as we unfold its successor states, but *all* trajectories in E, subject to the controlling influence of M must return it to *goal*. There may in fact be many cycles of differing length passing through the same goal state. Considering for the moment only the successor relation, E, We can express this as the modal necessity. For a state to be stable *every* successor state must either be the target or must in turn be stable. In the rules below, N is a variable.

$$\Box_E(@_N \vee stable(N)) \implies stable(N) \tag{1}$$

For the robot to successfully control the system of which it is a part, there need only be one possible motor action in M available to it in a given state. We're not concerned here with the exact timing of actions, but we assume a window in time exists during which such motor actions can be performed. If no motor action is taken then inevitably, and arbitrarily from the robot's perspective, one of the environmental transitions will eventually occur.

$$\Diamond_M(@_N \vee stable(N)) \implies stable(N) \tag{2}$$

The model is checked by querying if $stable(N)$ is true in the goal state.

For a more complex robot with internal state, or non-deterministic behaviour, M-cycles must be permitted. As it stands, the stability rule (2) would incorrectly reason that the model was stable. A slightly more sophisticated rule must be put in place to prevent these cycles being mistaken for stable equilibria. To overcome this we would ensure that every stable path must pass through at least one E-transition; the environment must have its turn in the game.

4 Model Checking

A Kripke *frame* $\langle W, R \rangle$ defines a non-empty set of possible worlds, W. These worlds are then linked together using the modal connectives E and M. R maps E and M to a binary relation on the the set of worlds known as an accessibility relation. The frame therefore defines an interpretation for the edges of the graph.

A distinctive feature of Kripke models is that each world is labeled by a number of propositions. This is defined by a *valuation* function, V, that maps each proposition P to a subset of W; the worlds in which P is true. This defines an interpretation for the nodes of the graph such that (W, R, V) is a model over the frame $\langle W, R \rangle$. Initially this valuation represents the envisionment process, the space of all possible combinations of the propositions *Left*, *Right*, *On*, *Off*, and *Lost*. However, as we are exploring and expanding the Kripke model by hand there is no need to expand unpromising dead-ends; only the model-checking process is automatic. It is sufficient to consider all successor states of states of interest. A guard prevents the expansion of rules (1) & (2) in worlds with no successor states, in this case the two *Lost* worlds.

Taking into consideration all the constraints on the model for the line-following robot into account, the Kripke model of Fig. 4 can be produced. The

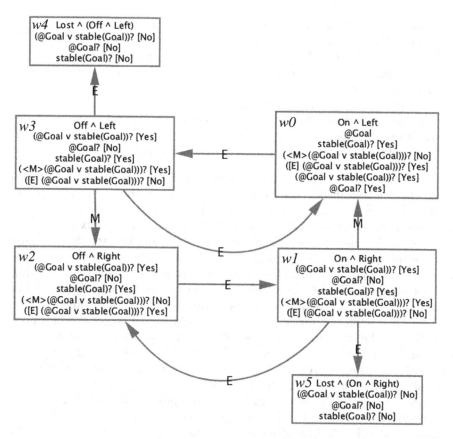

Fig. 4. Kripke model of the qualitative states of the line-following robot. Accessibility relation M denotes transitions caused directly by the robot, and relation E denotes transitions caused by the robot's environment. World $w0$ is initially identified as a representative '@Goal' state. Worlds $w0..w3$ define a stable region, so following inference both @Goal and stable(Goal) are true in $w0$. This indicates the presence of the stable region containing the goal.

model doesn't represent all possible actions that the robot could perform, but only those actions represented by the code of Fig. 2. Given that this is a reactive robot, there is at most one possible motor action from each state. However, we must consider things that could happen if the robot doesn't react in time. If it crosses the line but fails to switch heading, it will come about, turning through a full-circle to cross back across the line. This gives rise to the E transitions returning from $w3$ to $w0$, and from $w1$ to $w2$. While this may form a cycle through the goal state, it is not ultimately stable because of the transition from $w3$ to $w4$. Physically, this would correspond to the fact that the circular path is not perfectly circular and would eventually precess away from the edge. This model has the following features discussed earlier.

- World $w0$ is identified as the goal state with the nominal $@_{goal}$.
- Propositions *On* and *Off* describe the environmental input to the robot.
- Propositions *Left* and *Right* describe the motor actions of the robot.
- Modal connectives E & M represent environmental and motor (external and internal) transitions.
- For a *reactive* robot there can be no M-cycles.
- Without corrective motor action, the robot can potentially turn full circle, $w3$ to $w0$ or $w1$ to $w2$.
- The *Lost* worlds $w4$, & $w5$ are partial and unexplored.

The model-checking process takes this finite Kripke model as input, a specific world that we identified as our goal state identified by the nominal $@_{goal}$, and checks if a given formula $stable(goal)$ is true in that world. In LoTREC, a query is represented by a connective shown in Fig. 4 that adds a '?' suffix to the query proposition. The initial rule strategy unpacks this query in a top-down manner and the sub-queries fan out through the graph via the modal connectives. The model checking process eliminates the *necessity* or *possibility* operators by propagating the propositional content to a successor world, following the E and M connectives. The process of propagation terminates when the model saturates or it terminates when it reaches a successor world named $@_{goal}$, at which point it has closed the loop. However, it is not enough to find a *single* path back to the origin, but one or both of rules (1) & (2) must be satisfied throughout to ensure that a stable field exists. Note that in LoTREC atoms are capitalised, so '@Goal' is equivalent to '$@_{goal}$' in this context.

Once a query has been unpacked, the final proof is constructed from the bottom-up. This final stage of bottom-up model-checking is presented here as a natural proof in Fig. 5. The initial assertions include the definition of the accessibility relations (1–8) for the modal operators E and M, and the definition of rules (1) & (2). For the purposes of the proof, the worlds in Fig. 4 are labeled, $w0, w1, ...w5$. A modal operator $T(P, w)$ is used to assert the truth of a proposition P in world w, which is used initially to assert the nominal $@_{goal}$ in world $w0$. The object of the proof is to show that the goal state identified as $@_{goal}$ is within a stable region, such that all paths taken by the environment can be redirected back to the goal state via suitable motor actions, $T(@_{goal} \land stable(goal), w0)$.

The proof proceeds by conjunction and disjunction introduction ($\land$I & $\lor$I), necessity and possibility introduction ($\Box$I & $\Diamond$I), and implication elimination ($\Rightarrow$E). Implication elimination permits the application of rules (1) & (2). The possibility $\Diamond_M P$ can be introduced where there is at least one world accessible via M from the world identified in the T operator, where P is true. A good example of this is in step 13, where from world $w1$ it is possible to access world $w0$ in which $@_{goal} \land stable(goal)$ is true. In contrast, the necessity $\Box_E P$ may only be introduced where in *all* worlds accessible via E from the world identified in the T operator, P is true. A good example of this is step 16, where from world $w2$ we must consider successor state $w1$ to establish the necessity of $@_{goal} \land stable(goal)$.

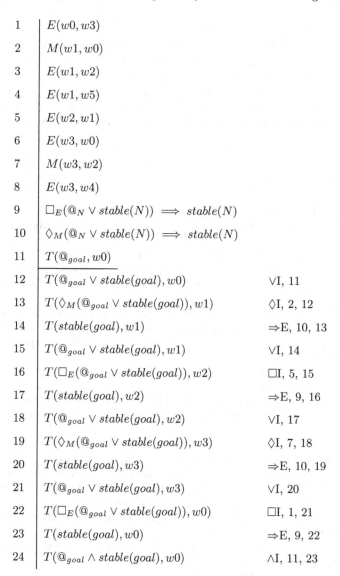

1	$E(w0, w3)$	
2	$M(w1, w0)$	
3	$E(w1, w2)$	
4	$E(w1, w5)$	
5	$E(w2, w1)$	
6	$E(w3, w0)$	
7	$M(w3, w2)$	
8	$E(w3, w4)$	
9	$\Box_E(@_N \vee stable(N)) \implies stable(N)$	
10	$\Diamond_M(@_N \vee stable(N)) \implies stable(N)$	
11	$T(@_{goal}, w0)$	
12	$T(@_{goal} \vee stable(goal), w0)$	$\vee$I, 11
13	$T(\Diamond_M(@_{goal} \vee stable(goal)), w1)$	$\Diamond$I, 2, 12
14	$T(stable(goal), w1)$	$\Rightarrow$E, 10, 13
15	$T(@_{goal} \vee stable(goal), w1)$	$\vee$I, 14
16	$T(\Box_E(@_{goal} \vee stable(goal)), w2)$	$\Box$I, 5, 15
17	$T(stable(goal), w2)$	$\Rightarrow$E, 9, 16
18	$T(@_{goal} \vee stable(goal), w2)$	$\vee$I, 17
19	$T(\Diamond_M(@_{goal} \vee stable(goal)), w3)$	$\Diamond$I, 7, 18
20	$T(stable(goal), w3)$	$\Rightarrow$E, 10, 19
21	$T(@_{goal} \vee stable(goal), w3)$	$\vee$I, 20
22	$T(\Box_E(@_{goal} \vee stable(goal)), w0)$	$\Box$I, 1, 21
23	$T(stable(goal), w0)$	$\Rightarrow$E, 9, 22
24	$T(@_{goal} \wedge stable(goal), w0)$	$\wedge$I, 11, 23

Fig. 5. Natural proof that the goal state identified as $@_{goal}$ is within a stable region.

5   Conclusion

Kripke models and tools such as LoTREC provide a powerful method for reasoning about stateful systems and provide the basis for automated model checking. Robot dynamics are a fruitful line of research that demonstrate how modal logic can be applied as a pragmatic tool for analysing the qualitative state space of a robot coupled with its environment. In this application, modal logic appears to be particularly apt, as the concept of *necessity* allows us to reason about the field flow as a whole rather than focusing on individual trajectories. On the other hand, the concept of *possibility* injects a way to directly control the system, allowing the robot to steer it towards a goal state. Only two modal operators are required to distinguish state variables under direct control of the robot, from those it is able to influence only indirectly, such as its position. These operators allow analysis of the behavioural model checking not only for cyclicity, but also for stability.

References

1. Ashby, W.: Design for a Brain. Chapman and Hall, London (1960)
2. Ashby, W.R.: An Introduction to Cybernetics. Chapman and Hall Ltd., London (1956)
3. Forbus, K.D.: Qualitative Process Theory. MIT AI Lab Memo, Cambridge (1982)
4. Forbus, K.D.: Qualitative physics: past, present, and future. In: Exploring Artificial Intelligence, chap. 7, pp. 239–296. Morgan-Kaufmann Publishers Inc., San Francisco (1988)
5. Harel, D., Kantor, A.: Modal scenarios as automata. In: Dershowitz, N., Nissan, E. (eds.) Language, Culture, Computation. Computing - Theory and Technology. LNCS, vol. 8001, pp. 156–167. Springer, Heidelberg (2014). https://doi.org/10.1007/978-3-642-45321-2_7
6. De Kleer, J.: Qualitative and quantitative knowledge in classical mechanics. Technical report 352 (1975)
7. Kripke, S.A.: Semantical analysis of modal logic in normal propositional calculi. Zeitschrift fur mathematische Logik und Grundlagen der Mathematik **9**(56), 67–96 (1963)
8. Kuipers, B.: Qualitative simulation. Artif. Intell. **29**, 289–338 (2001)
9. del Cerro, L.F., Fauthoux, D., Gasquet, O., Herzig, A., Longin, D., Massacci, F.: Lotrec: the generic tableau prover for modal and description logics. In: Goré, R., Leitsch, A., Nipkow, T. (eds.) IJCAR 2001. LNCS, vol. 2083, pp. 453–458. Springer, Heidelberg (2001). https://doi.org/10.1007/3-540-45744-5_38
10. Pask, G.: An Approach to Cybernetics. Hutchinson Science Library. Harper, New York (1961)
11. Pnueli, A.: The temporal logic of programs. In: Proceedings of the 18th Annual Symposium on Foundations of Computer Science, SFCS 1977, pp. 46–57. IEEE Computer Society, Washington, DC (1977)
12. Prior, A.N.: Papers on Time and Tense. Oxford University Press, Oxford (2003)
13. Santos, F., Carmo, J.: Indirect action, influence and responsibility. In: Brown, M.A., Carmo, J. (eds.) Deontic Logic, Agency and Normative Systems. WC, pp. 194–215. Springer, London (1996). https://doi.org/10.1007/978-1-4471-1488-8_11
14. van Diggelen, J.: Using modal logic in mobile robots. Ph.D. thesis, Utrecht University (2002)
15. Vardi, M.Y., Wolper, P.: Reasoning about infinite computations. Inf. Comput. **115**, 1–37 (1994)

16. Wiley, T., Sammut, C., Bratko, I.: Qualitative planning with quantitative constraints for online learning of robotic behaviours. In: Brodley, C.E., Stone, P. (eds.) AAAI, pp. 2578–2584. AAAI Press (2014)
17. Yershova, A., Tovar, B., Ghrist, R., LaValle, S.M.: Bitbots: simple robots solving complex tasks. In: Proceedings of the 20th National Conference on Artificial Intelligence, AAAI 2005, vol. 3, pp. 1336–1341. AAAI Press (2005)

Bio-inspired Problem Solving

The Self-Generating Model:
An Adaptation of the Self-organizing Map
for Intelligent Agents and Data Mining

Amy de Buitléir$^{(\boxtimes)}$ ⓘ, Mark Daly, and Michael Russell

Faculty of Engineering and Informatics, Athlone Institute of Technology,
Athlone, Ireland
amy@nualeargais.ie, {mdaly,mrussell}@ait.ie

Abstract. We present the Self-Generating Model (SGM), a new version of the Self-organizing Map (SOM) that has been adapted for use in intelligent data mining ALife agents. The SGM sacrifices the topology-preserving ability of the SOM, but is equally accurate, and faster, at identifying handwritten numerals. It achieves a higher accuracy faster than the SOM. Furthermore, it increases model stability and reduces the problem of "wasted" models. We feel that the SGM could be a useful alternative to the SOM when topology preservation is not required.

Keywords: Self-organizing map · Artificial life · Intelligent agents

1 Introduction

Data mining is the extraction of insights from data. In contrast with an ordinary database search or query, where the key features and relationships are known; in data mining, they have to be discovered [1, p. 5].

Data mining includes a wide range of tasks. *Landscape mining* explores the data to find the space of possible inferences (the data's "landscape") and to identify interesting patterns before leaping in with more traditional data analysis tools [2]. *Classification* assigns objects to predefined categories based on the attributes of the objects [3]. *Clustering* (also known as unsupervised classification or exploratory data analysis) partitions items into a set of clusters such that items within a cluster have similar characteristics, and items in different clusters have different characteristics [3,4]. *Prediction* (also known as forecasting) estimates future (or unknown) data based on present data and past trends, validating hypotheses [3,5, p. 4]. *Regression* identifies functions which map data objects to prediction variables [3,5, p. 4]. *Modelling* produces a (typically simpler) representation of the data that captures important features and relationships. Such models can be used for classification, prediction, and to provide insight about the data. *Visualisation* makes insights understandable by humans [3].

The self-organizing map (SOM) provides a way to represent high-dimensional data in fewer dimensions (typically two), while preserving the topology of the

© Springer International Publishing AG, part of Springer Nature 2018
P. R. Lewis et al. (Eds.): ALIA 2016, CCIS 732, pp. 59–72, 2018.
https://doi.org/10.1007/978-3-319-90418-4_5

input data [6]. The SOM is a set of models associated with nodes in a regular grid. Patterns that are similar to each other in the high-dimensional space are mapped to models that are near each other on the grid. (There are exceptions to this topology-preserving property, however; see Villmann et al. [7].)

In addition to topology preservation, SOMs have benefits that make them useful for artificial life (ALife) and intelligent agents. They are easy to understand and implement. The SOM models can be inspected directly, which makes it easier to debug problems with the implementation or the learning function. After a SOM has been trained, labels can be assigned to the nodes to allow it to be used for classification. It can also be used to cluster data; a U-matrix (whose elements are the Euclidean distance between neighbouring cells) will have high values at the cluster edges [8].

SOMs have an established place in the data mining tool set, especially for clustering and classification. They have also been used, often with modifications, in ALife [9,10]. and artificial intelligence [11,12]. de Buitléir et al. [13] described an ALife species designed for data mining, called *wains*. Wains live in, and subsist on, data; data mining is their survival problem. Their brains use modified SOMs to model their environment and to identify patterns in the data. Wains were originally used with images of handwritten numerals [13], but they have also been applied to the task of speech recognition, identifying audio samples of spoken numerals [14,15].

In this paper we present the Self-Generating Model (SGM), a new version of the SOM that is modified for use by intelligent agents. However, the modifications may be useful in other applications as well. We will describe the traditional SOM and historical modifications to it (Sect. 2), discuss the goals of our modifications (Sect. 3), describe the SGM algorithm (Sect. 4), discuss the experimental set-up (Sect. 5), compare the behaviour of the SOM and the SGM (Sect. 6) and present our conclusions (Sect. 7).

2   The SOM Algorithm

SOM training (see Algorithm 1) is unsupervised. The elements (patterns) of the input data are typically numeric vectors, but they can be any data type so long as we can define a measurement of similarity between two patterns, and a method to make one pattern more similar to another, by an arbitrary amount. The SOM models are arranged on a (typically two-dimensional) grid of fixed size. The models must be initialised.

Step 3 ensures that as additional input patterns are received, nodes that are physically close respond to similar patterns in the input data. Thus, the resulting grid preserves the topology of the original high-dimensional data. SOMs "translate *data similarities* into *spatial relationships*" (emphasis in the original) [16].

The traditional SOM has been adapted and extended in many ways. Common modifications include use of grids in non-euclidean spaces [16], dynamically increasing the size of the grid [17], replacing the grid with a hierarchical arrangement of nodes [18], and combining with principal component analysis [19]. There is extensive literature on SOMs with two or more of these modifications [20–27].

Algorithm 1. SOM algorithm.

For each input pattern,

1. Compare the input pattern to all models in the SOM. The node with the model that is most similar to the input pattern is called the *winning node*.
2. The winning node's model is adjusted to make it slightly more similar to the input pattern. The amount of adjustment is determined by the learning rate, which typically decays over time.
3. The models of all nodes within a given radius of the winning node are also adjusted to make them slightly more similar to the input pattern, by an amount which is smaller the further the node is from the winning node.

3 Adapting the SOM for Intelligent Data Mining ALife Agents

The requirements for a classifier used in intelligent data mining ALife agents are rather different than for more common applications. For example, in recognising handwritten or spoken numerals, it is not necessary to preserve the topology of the input data set. (We may not be interested in knowing whether a particular '3' is more similar to an '8' or a '6'.) In an early implementation of wains, de Buitléir et al. [13] made a small modification to the SOM to improve performance. By updating only the winning node, the topology-preserving ability of the SOM was sacrificed in favour of speed [13].

If we dispense with topology preservation, what is the cost? Consider that in addition to a SOM-like classifier, the brain of an intelligent data mining ALife agent might include a mechanism that uses the information provided by the classifier to determine what response to take. This is the approach used by de Buitléir et al. [13]. For convenience, we'll call this mechanism the *decider*. Suppose that the classifier assigns the label a to the current scenario, and the decider does not know a good response to a. If the classifier preserves the topology of the input data, the decider can look for the nearest neighbour of a for which it *does* know a good response, and choose that (see Fig. 1). If a good response to a neighbour of a is likely to be a good response to a, this tactic could benefit the agent's survival.

However, there may be other ways to achieve the same result. The classifier could report the similarity of the scenario to *all* models, including the model labelled a. (This information is calculated anyway as part of the SOM algorithm.) Without needing to know anything about the topology used by the classifier, the decider can look for known responses to models that are similar, and choose a response that is known to be good for a similar model (see Fig. 2). Thus, we can sacrifice topology preservation in favour of other goals.

One advantage of the SOM for intelligent agents is that the models can be extracted from the classifier, making it easier to understand how an agent perceives the object, and evaluate any decisions the agent makes in response. This is a feature we wanted to keep. In a traditional neural net, it can be difficult or even impossible to analyse why the net makes certain classifications.

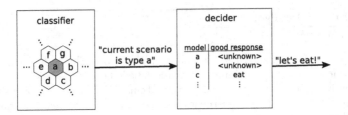

Fig. 1. Decision-making using a classifier that preserves topology.

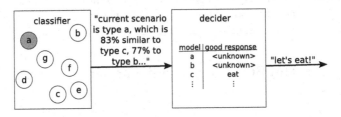

Fig. 2. Decision-making using a classifier that uses disconnected models and does not preserve topology.

Many SOM modifications are motivated by a desire for greater accuracy in classifying; however, this may not be necessary for some agent implementations. In a multi-agent system one can ask the same question of multiple agents, each with a different set of lifetime experiences, to get independent opinions. By averaging the responses, a "wisdom of the crowd" effect could produce greater accuracy than a single agent could achieve. Thus, increasing accuracy was not one of our goals.

However, we did have a goal of **early accuracy**. Agents cannot wait until they have a full, final set of models (they continue to learn throughout their lives) to begin learning rules for survival. Agents need to be able to "hit the ground running". An agent should have a useful, if small, set of models early in life; this will allow it to experiment with possible responses to objects in their environment, and to learn from the results.

Another goal in adapting the SOM was to have **stable models.** Agents make decisions based on the patterns that they encounter, and the mental categories (node labels) associated with the patterns. Agents experiment by trying different actions in response to each cluster of patterns. Through trial and error, each agent develops rules that select the appropriate action to take in response to each pattern cluster. If models change to such a degree that they no longer match patterns that they used to match, agents may need to "unlearn" existing rules and replace them with new ones.

As will be shown, SOM models can be very unstable. This can make it more difficult for agents to learn appropriate responses for their environment. For example, suppose the environment has both edible and poisonous berries; and an agent can distinguish by some characteristic such as colour. We would expect an agent to develop at least one model that matches edible berries but not poisonous ones. The agent has a better chance of surviving if it learns to eat objects that match this model. Now imagine that the model changes so much that it now matches the poisonous berries. The eating response that the agent has learned is now dangerous. In order to survive, the agent must "unlearn" the eating response and learn a more appropriate action. The situation is even worse if the model changes from matching poisonous berries to edible ones. The agent may have ruled out eating anything that matches this model, and may never try eating the edible berries.

Once those goals are met, there are additional features that would be desirable in a modified SOM. We want a **faster algorithm**; this can be achieved if we **minimise what we call "wasted" models**. Models that will can not be used to classify future patterns are wasted; the computational effort to create and update those models is unnecessary. This is especially important because instead of working with a single SOM, we may require a population of agents with SOMs in their brains, thus amplifying any inefficiencies in the algorithm.

Finally, we hope to use the modified SOM in a variety of data mining applications. Therefore, we wanted a **generic algorithm**, not one that was tailored to a specific type of data such as images or audio samples.

Why not modify the SOM, when other classifier algorithms are available that are also capable of unsupervised learning? It is often impractical for an agent to keep a copy of every data input it has encountered during its life; fortunately SOMs only require that we keep the models. Contrast this with an algorithm such as k-means which requires that we re-calculate the centroid at each step, accessing all of the data seen previously [4]. Particle Swarm Optimisation (PSO) similarly iterates over all the data, making it unsuitable for this application [28].

Learning Classifier Systems (LCSs) [29, Sect. 3.9] learn the best action to take in response to a set of conditions. As such, the LCS might be suitable as a replacement for *both* the classification and decision-making components in a wain (as we will discuss in Sect. 7). However, it seems overkill to replace just the classifier with an LCS. Finally, as mentioned earlier, SOM models can be inspected directly. A trained neural network stores what it has learned as weights [4]; making it difficult to extract the models.

4   Self-Generating Model

To satisfy the above goals, we adapted the basic SOM algorithm to produce the SGM algorithm (see Algorithm 2). The SGM can be initially empty, or it can be initialised with a set of (possibly random) models. Step 2, adjusting the winning node, has been modified to allow the classifier to grow as needed and produce models that are useful as soon as they are created. In addition, Step 3 of the SOM algorithm, adjusting models in the neighbourhood of the winning node, has been eliminated in an attempt to improve performance, and to minimise wasted models. The *difference threshold* helps to ensure that models do not change too much during the lifetime of the SGM, providing model stability Like the SOM, the SGM design is generic; it has not been tailored to a specific kind of data.

Algorithm 2. SGM algorithm.

For each input pattern,

1. Compare the input pattern to all models in the SGM. The node with the model that is most similar to the input pattern is called the *winning node*.
2. If the difference between the input pattern and the winning node's model is greater than the *difference threshold*, and the SGM is not at capacity (number of models < maximum), a new model is created that is identical to the input pattern. Otherwise, the winning node's model is adjusted to make it slightly more similar to the input pattern. The amount of adjustment is determined by the learning rate, which typically decays over time.

5   Experimental Set-up

The experiments described in this paper used the MNIST database, which is a collection of images of hand-written numerals from Census Bureau employees and high-school students [30]. The training set contains 60,000 images, while the test set contains 10,000 images. All images are 28 × 28 pixels, and are grey-scale as a result of anti-aliasing. The centre of pixel mass of the numeral has been placed in the centre of the image. Sample images are shown in Fig. 3. We used the database images without modification.

Fig. 3. Sample images from the MNIST database [30].

For all experiments, the SOM used the learning function given by Eq. 1,

$$f(d, t) = r e^{-\frac{d^2}{2w^2}}, \tag{1}$$

where

$$r = r_0 \left(\frac{r_f}{r_0}\right)^a, \quad w = w_0 \left(\frac{w_f}{w_0}\right)^a, \quad \text{and} \quad a = \frac{t}{t_f}.$$

The parameter r_0 is the initial learning rate, r_f is the learning rate at time t_f, w_0 is the radius of the initial neighbourhood, and w_f is the radius of the neighbourhood at time t_f. For the winning node, $d = 0$, and Eq. 1 reduces to Eq. 2,

$$f(t) = r = r_0 \left(\frac{r_f}{r_0}\right)^a. \tag{2}$$

We used Eq. 2 as the learning function for the SGM in all experiments. Thus, at all times the learning rate of the SGM matches the learning rate of the winning node in the SOM. This permits a fairer comparison of the SOM and the SGM.

We use the Mean of Absolute Differences (MAD) as a measure of difference between two images. The absolute difference between each pair of corresponding pixels in the two images is calculated and the mean taken, to obtain a number between 0 (identical) and 1 (maximally dissimilar). As all the images in the MNIST database have the same size, viewing direction (normal to the plane of the image, from above), and comparable intensity, the MAD is an appropriate difference metric.

The models for each SOM were initialised with images containing random low pixel values similar to the background of the MNIST images. Each SGM was initially empty, having no nodes or models.

Once a classifier has been trained, the nodes must be labelled with the numeral represented by the associated model before the classifier can be used for testing. To do this, we counted the number of times each node was the winning node for each numeral during the training phase. The node was then labelled with the numeral it most often matched.

5.1 Experiment 1: Early Accuracy

Recall that agents cannot wait until they have a full, final set of models to begin learning appropriate responses. This experiment determines how long it takes to develop a useful, if small, set of models. For this experiment, we used a SOM and SGM of similar size. After 25 training images, chosen at random, had been presented to a classifier, we tested its accuracy with the entire test set, presented in random order. We repeated the process with various amounts of training, from 50 up to 500 images.

Table 1 shows the configuration of the classifiers for this experiment. The values r_0 and r_f were chosen so that the learning rate would start at maximum and be near zero by the end of training. The values w_0 and w_f were chosen through experimentation. The value of t_f is the number of training images.

Recall that if the difference between an input pattern and the winning node's model is greater than the difference threshold, and the SGM is not at capacity, a

Table 1. Configuration of SOM and SGM in Experiment 1

Variable	SOM	SGM
Node count	100	96
Grid type	Rectangular	Unconnected nodes
r_0	1	1
r_f	1×10^{-4}	1×10^{-4}
w_0	2	Not applicable
w_f	1×10^{-4}	Not applicable
t_f	60000	60000
Difference threshold	Not applicable	0.165

new model is created. Once capacity is reached, the SGM will always update the most similar model, which increases the chance of a model eventually representing a different numeral than it was created for. We wanted to compare the SGM with a small (10×10) SOM. However, an SGM may not create the maximum number of models. In order to maximise model stability, we used an SGM with a maximum capacity of 2000 models, and relied on the difference threshold to indirectly control the number of models created.

To find a reasonable value for this difference threshold, we selected a random set of 500 images and measured the MAD between all pairs of images. The results are shown in Table 2. Experimenting with the values near the two means, we discovered that a threshold of 0.165 resulted in the SGM creating 96 models, which was useful for comparison with the 100 models in the SOM.

Table 2. Analysis of MAD between MNIST images, based on a sample of 500 images. The first column contains the *mean of the mean* absolute difference; the second, the *standard deviation of the mean.*

	Mean	Std. dev.
Same numeral	0.135	0.0436
Different numerals	0.171	0.0374

5.2   Experiment 2: Full Training Run

To compare the overall accuracy of the SOM and SGM, we created a randomised list of all 60,000 images in the MNIST training set. The training images were then presented, in this order, to a small and large SOM, and a small and large

Table 3. Configuration of SOM and SGM in Experiment 2

Variable	SOM	SGM
Grid size	$4 \times 4, 6 \times 6, 8 \times 8, 10 \times 10, 15 \times 15,$ $20 \times 20, 25 \times 25, 30 \times 30, 35 \times 35,$ $40 \times 40, 45 \times 45, 70 \times 70$	Initially empty, grows as needed
Grid type	Rectangular	Unconnected nodes
r_0	0.1	0.1
r_f	1×10^{-4}	1×10^{-4}
w_0	2	Not applicable
w_f	1×10^{-4}	Not applicable
t_f	60000	60000
Difference threshold	Not applicable	0.09, 0.1, 0.105, 0.11, 0.115, 0.12, 0.13, 0.14, 0.15, 0.16, 0.17, 0.18, 0.19, 0.2, 0.21

SGM. Next, we created a randomised list of all 10,000 images in the test set, and presented those to the SOM and the SGM for classification. This allowed us to compare the accuracy, speed, model stability and number of wasted models for the two classifiers.

Table 3 shows the configuration of the classifiers for this experiment. In preliminary trials, we found that the accuracy of both the SOM and the SGM depends strongly on the number of models, weakly on r_0, and very weakly on the other configuration parameters. Therefore, for this experiment we chose to vary the classifier size, while keeping r_0 and r_f constant. The values r_0 and r_f were chosen so that the learning rate would start at maximum and be near zero by the end of training. The values w_0 and w_f were chosen through experimentation. The value of t_f is the number of training images.

6 Results and Interpretation

6.1 Experiment 1: Early Accuracy

Figure 4 compares the accuracy of the SOM and SGM during the early part of training. The SGM reaches a usable level of accuracy faster than the SOM.

6.2 Experiment 2: Full Training Run

Figures 5 and 6 show one pair of small classifier models after all of the training images have been presented to the small classifiers. From Fig. 5 we can see that many of the models are blurry combinations of more than one numeral. The topology of the input data has been partially preserved; models of the same numeral tend to be near each other.

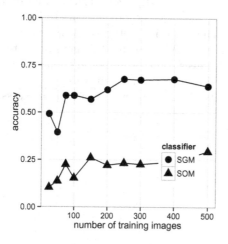

Fig. 4. Early accuracy comparison

There are four shaded models in Fig. 5. They were not winning nodes at any point during testing, were not used to classify testing images and are counted as "wasted". An unmatched model could be assigned the same label as was assigned to a majority of its neighbours. However, this would result in the left pair of unmatched models (shaded) being assigned labels for the numeral '1', even though they are clearly better matches for '0'. The right pair of unmatched models are very ambiguous; it may be better not to use them.

Figure 6 shows the small SGM after training. We can see that the topology has not been preserved. Unfortunately, there are still many ambiguous models, perhaps due to the small size of the classifier.

Figure 7 compares model stability for the SOM and SGM. To measure this, we noted the first numeral matched by the model. (In the case of an SGM, this is the numeral the model was created in response to.) We compared this to the numeral used to label the model's node (at the end of training). If the numerals were the same, we counted the model as stable. The SGM consistently achieved higher model stability.

Figure 8 compares model usage. A model is counted as "used" if it was the winning node at any point during testing, otherwise it is considered "wasted". The SGM consistently used more of its models, reducing the problem of wasted models.

Figure 9 shows the time required for training and testing the SOM and SGM. For all but the smallest classifiers, the SGM is considerably faster than the SOM. We believe the reduction in processing time occurs primarily because the SGM only updates one model during training, while the SOM updates the models in the neighbourhood of the winning node. In addition, the SGM has fewer models during the early part of training, and therefore does not need to make as many comparisons as the SOM does.

Figure 10 compares the accuracy of the classifiers. The accuracy is the number of times that an image was correctly identified, divided by the total number of images. The accuracy of the two methods appears to be comparable. For all but the smallest SOMs, a small fraction of the nodes were not winning nodes at any point during training. We could have labelled these nodes to match the majority of their neighbours. However, there were not enough to significantly impact the accuracy, so we counted them as correct answers.

The code and results for this experiment are open access [31,32]

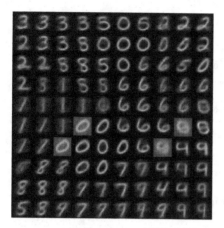

Fig. 5. Small SOM after all 60,000 training images have been presented. Models are arranged in a grid. Wasted models are shaded.

Fig. 6. Small SGM after all 60,000 training images have been presented. Models are unconnected; they are shown here in the order they were created. There were no wasted models.

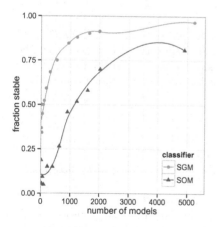

Fig. 7. Model stability. Larger values are better. The lines show a loess (local polynomial regression) data fit.

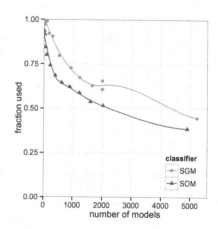

Fig. 8. Model usage. Larger values are better. The lines show a loess (local polynomial regression) data fit.

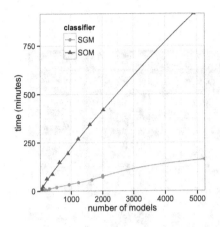

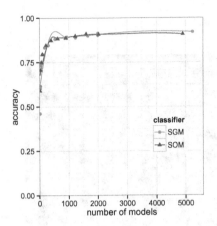

Fig. 9. Processing time. Smaller values are better. The lines show a loess (local polynomial regression) data fit.

Fig. 10. Accuracy. Larger values are better. The lines show a loess (local polynomial regression) data fit.

7   Conclusions

The overall accuracy of the two classifiers is comparable, but the SGM achieves a higher accuracy faster. This could allow an agent to make good survival decisions with less training. In the SGM, model stability was higher. Furthermore, the SGM significantly reduces wasted models, making it faster than the SOM. We feel that the SGM could be a useful component for implementing intelligent agents. Furthermore, it may be useful for other clustering or classification applications.

Areas for future research include comparing the accuracy of the SOM and SGM on other types of data (e.g., audio), and designing a brain based on the SGM that would allow an agent to learn to survive in an environment through experimentation. The new brain design could be compared to both the existing design for the wain, and to an LCS.

References

1. Gorunescu, F.: Data mining concepts, models and techniques (2011). http://site.ebrary.com/id/10454853
2. Menzies, T.: Beyond data mining. IEEE Softw. **30**(3), 92 (2013)
3. Goebel, M., Gruenwald, L.: A survey of data mining and knowledge discovery software tools. ACM SIGKDD Explor. Newsl. **1**(1), 20–33 (1999). http://www.lcb.uu.se/users/janko/data/goebel_sigkddexp99.pdf
4. Xu, R., Wunsch, D.: Survey of clustering algorithms. IEEE Trans. Neural Netw. **16**(3), 645–678 (2005). http://ieeexplore.ieee.org/xpl/articleDetails.jsp?arnumber=1427769

5. Fayyad, U.M.: Advances in Knowledge Discovery and Data Mining (American Association for Artificial Intelligence). MIT Press, Cambridge (1996). http://www.amazon.co.uk/dp/0262560976
6. Kohonen, T.: Self-Organizing Maps. Springer Series in Information Sciences, vol. 30, 3rd edn. Springer, Heidelberg (2001). https://doi.org/10.1007/978-3-642-56927-2. http://www.worldcat.org/isbn/3540679219
7. Villmann, T., Der, R., Herrmann, M., Martinetz, T.: Topology preservation in self-organizing feature maps: exact definition and measurement. IEEE Trans. Neural Netw. **8**(2), 256–266 (1997). http://ieeexplore.ieee.org/xpl/articleDetails.jsp?arnumber=557663
8. Ultsch, A., Siemon, H.P.: Kohonen's self organizing feature maps for exploratory data analysis. In: Widrow, B., Angeniol, B. (eds.) Proceedings of the International Neural Network Conference (INNC 1990), Paris, France, 9–13 July 1990, vol. 1, pp. 305–308. Kluwer Academic Press, Dordrecht (1990). http://www.uni-marburg.de/fb12/datenbionik/pdf/pubs/1990/UltschSiemon90
9. Saunders, R., Gero, J.S.: Artificial creativity: a synthetic approach to the study of creative behaviour. In: Computational and Cognitive Models of Creative Design V, Key Centre of Design Computing and Cognition, University of Sydney, Sydney, pp. 113–139 (2001)
10. Martins, J.M., Miranda, E.R.: A connectionist architecture for the evolution of rhythms. In: Rothlauf, F., et al. (eds.) EvoWorkshops 2006. LNCS, vol. 3907, pp. 696–706. Springer, Heidelberg (2006). https://doi.org/10.1007/11732242_66
11. Riga, T., Cangelosi, A., Greco, A.: Symbol grounding transfer with hybrid self-organizing/supervised neural networks. In: Proceedings of the 2004 IEEE International Joint Conference on Neural Networks, vol. 4, pp. 2865–2869. IEEE (2004)
12. Saunders, R., Gemeinboeck, P., Lombard, A., Bourke, D., Kocabali, B.: Curious whispers: an embodied artificial creative system. In: International Conference on Computational Creativity, pp. 7–9 (2010)
13. de Buitléir, A., Russell, M., Daly, M.: Wains: a pattern-seeking artificial life species. Artif. Life **18**(4), 399–423 (2012)
14. Salaja, R.T., Flynn, R., Russell, M.: Automatic speech recognition using artificial life. In: 25th IET Irish Signals and Systems Conference 2014 and 2014 China-Ireland International Conference on Information and Communities Technologies (ISSC 2014/CIICT 2014). Institution of Engineering and Technology (IET) (2014). https://doi.org/10.1049/cp.2014.0665
15. Salaja, R.T., Flynn, R., Russell, M.: Evaluation of Wains as a classifier for automatic speech recognition. In: 2015 26th Irish Signals and Systems Conference (ISSC), pp. 1–6, June 2015. http://ieeexplore.ieee.org/xpl/articleDetails.jsp?arnumber=7163770
16. Ritter, H.: Self-organizing maps on non-Euclidean spaces. Kohonen Maps **73**, 97–110 (1999)
17. Alahakoon, D., Halgamuge, S.K., Srinivasan, B.: Dynamic self-organizing maps with controlled growth for knowledge discovery. IEEE Trans. Neural Netw. **11**(3), 601–614 (2000). http://ieeexplore.ieee.org/xpl/articleDetails.jsp?arnumber=846732
18. Koikkalainen, P., Oja, E.: Self-organizing hierarchical feature maps. In: 1990 IJCNN International Joint Conference on Neural Networks, vol. 2, pp. 279–284, June 1990
19. Kohonen, T.: The adaptive-subspace SOM (ASSOM) and its use for the implementation of invariant feature detection. In: Proceedings of ICANN 1995, pp. 3–10 (1995)

20. Batista, L.B., Gomes, H.M., Herbster, R.F.: Application of growing hierarchical self-organizing map in handwritten digit recognition. In: Proceedings of 16th Brazilian Symposium on Computer Graphics and Image Processing (SIBGRAPI), pp. 1539–1545 (2003)
21. Cecotti, H., Belaïd, A.: Rejection strategy for convolutional neural network by adaptive topology applied to handwritten digits recognition. In: Proceedings of Eighth International Conference on Document Analysis and Recognition, vol. 2, pp. 765–769, August 2005. http://ieeexplore.ieee.org/xpl/articleDetails.jsp?arnumber=1575648
22. Mohebi, E., Bagirov, A.: A convolutional recursive modified self organizing map for handwritten digits recognition. Neural Netw. **60**, 104–118 (2014). http://www.sciencedirect.com/science/article/pii/S0893608014001968
23. Ontrup, J., Ritter, H.: A hierarchically growing hyperbolic self-organizing map for rapid structuring of large data sets. In: Proceedings of the 5th Workshop on Self-Organizing Maps, Paris, France (2005)
24. Pakkanen, J.: The evolving tree, a new kind of self-organizing neural network. In: proceedings of the Workshop on Self-Organizing Maps, vol. 3, pp. 311–316. Citeseer (2003)
25. Rauber, A., Merkl, D., Dittenbach, M.: The growing hierarchical self-organizing map: exploratory analysis of high-dimensional data. IEEE Trans. Neural Netw. **13**(6), 1331–1341 (2002)
26. Shah-Hosseini, H.: Binary tree time adaptive self-organizing map. Neurocomputing **74**(11), 1823–1839 (2011). http://www.sciencedirect.com/science/article/pii/S0925231211000786. Adaptive Incremental Learning in Neural NetworksLearning Algorithm and Mathematic Modelling Selected papers from the International Conference on Neural Information Processing (ICONIP 2009)
27. Zheng, H., Shen, W., Dai, Q., Hu, S., Lu, Z.M.: Learning nonlinear manifolds based on mixtures of localized linear manifolds under a self-organizing framework. Neurocomputing **72**(1315), 3318–3330 (2009). http://www.sciencedirect.com/science/article/pii/S0925231209000605. Hybrid Learning Machines (HAIS 2007). Recent Developments in Natural Computation (ICNC 2007)
28. Van der Merwe, D., Engelbrecht, A.P.: Data clustering using particle swarm optimization. In: The 2003 Congress on Evolutionary Computation, CEC2003, vol. 1, pp. 215–220. IEEE (2003)
29. Brownlee, J.: Clever algorithms: nature-inspired programming recipes. Lulu (2011). http://www.worldcat.org/search?qt=worldcat_org_all&q=9781446785065
30. LeCun, Y., Cortes, C.: MNIST handwritten digit database (2010). http://yann.lecun.com/exdb/mnist/
31. de Buitléir, A.: Software release: SOM v9.0, January 2016. https://doi.org/10.5281/zenodo.45039
32. de Buitléir, A.: Exp-SOM-comparison v0.1.0.0, January 2016. https://doi.org/10.5281/zenodo.45040

A Grammar-Directed Heuristic Optimisation Algorithm and Comparisons with Grammatical Evolution on the Artificial Ant Problem

William J. Teahan$^{(\boxtimes)}$ (iD)

Bangor University, Wales, UK
w.j.teahan@bangor.ac.uk

Abstract. This paper describes a new heuristic search optimisation algorithm capable of automatically generating programs in any language as solutions to a problem using an arbitrary BNF-based grammar. The approach maintains two populations of agents: the first, a set of partially generated programs that are built as a result of the agents traversing in parallel the entire search space of possible programs as determined by the grammar; and the second, a set of completely generated programs that are tested to see how they perform in the problem. Both populations are updated during each iteration by using a fitness function to prune out poorly performing agents. The effectiveness of the algorithm is evaluated on variations of the Santa Fe Trail problem. Experimental results show that the algorithm is capable of finding the optimal solution of 165 steps (i.e. the path itself as described by the three move, left turn and right turn operators without any conditional operator) whereas the best solutions found by Genetic Programming and Grammatical Evolution typically involve several hundred more steps. When using a grammar that omits the conditional operator, the algorithm again finds the optimal solution, unlike Grammatical Evolution which finds no solution at all.

1 Background and Motivation

Evolutionary algorithms have shown great promise with their ability to find solutions to problems in many different domains. However, these solutions have in general been limited in complexity compared to what human problem solving and invention has achieved. Koza [3] has proposed increasingly more difficult criteria in order to measure the success of Genetic Programming (GP) with the ultimate criterion being the ability to generate completely new patentable inventions. Although notable successes have been achieved [4], the complexity of the type of problems tackled and the complexity of solutions that have been found are severely constrained by the limitations of the evolutionary algorithms used to find them. For example, the promise of a computer being able to write complex programs without human aid has still not eventuated. Often the programming language used in experiments is reduced to a small sub-language compared to

© Springer International Publishing AG, part of Springer Nature 2018
P. R. Lewis et al. (Eds.): ALIA 2016, CCIS 732, pp. 73–90, 2018.
https://doi.org/10.1007/978-3-319-90418-4_6

an unconstrained language such as Java or C++; and even then, finding solutions that involve hundreds and thousands of lines of code are beyond most evolutionary algorithms.

Grammatical Evolution (GE) is a relatively new type of evolutionary algorithm [5] whose approach has also shown much promise. It provides a means for clearly distinguishing between the genotype and phenotype by using a mapping to generate phenotypes (programs) from genotypes (populations of bitstrings) using a grammar that defines the syntax of allowable programs.

Our research wishes to push the boundaries of GE-related research as its properties appeal, such as the search space being clearly defined and constrained by the grammar, and we believe the algorithm has much potential. In this light, and in order to explore GE better, we have sought out situations where GE underperforms in order that we can explore possible improvements to GE and/or explore alternative approaches for these situations. This paper has arisen as the result of such research.

The rest of this paper is organised as follows. In the next section, we discuss the Santa Fe Trail problem that has become a standard benchmark used for comparing the performance of GP and GE algorithms and highlight several issues in relation to using the problem for benchmarking purposes. The paper then describes the new algorithm and the experimental results, with a conclusion and discussion in the final section.

2   Variations of the Santa Fe Trail Problem

The Santa Fe Trail problem designed by Christopher Langton [3, p. 54] is an example of the Artificial Ant problem often used to benchmark GP and GE algorithms. It consists of finding a set of instructions for an artificial ant that will enable it to find food along a trail set in a 32 by 32 environment, as shown on the right of Fig. 1. The ant starts at the top left, and must proceed along the trail (shown in the figure as dark green to represent food, and as brown to represent gaps in the trail where there is no food) incurring as few steps as possible along the way. The ant is limited in the actions it can perform—it can only perform three 'motor' actions, represented in NetLogo [8] as:

- move: The ant moves forward one step (fd 1).
- turn-left: The ant turns left by 90° (lt 90).
- turn-right: The ant turns right by 90° (rt 90).

In addition, the ant has a single 'sensing' action:

- food-ahead: This reports whether there is food directly ahead of the ant.

Artificial Ant Problems such as the Santa Fe Trail problem provide a useful challenge for evolutionary and automatic programming algorithms. However, one drawback is that it is unclear what the best solution is for the problem (in terms of the number of steps needed to traverse the trail, for example), and as

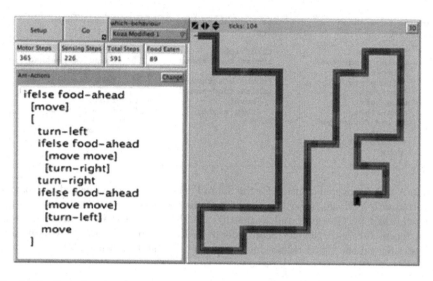

Fig. 1. The Interface for the Santa Fe Trail NetLogo model [6, p. 10] that was developed to test out solutions for the Santa Fe Trail. The trail is shown on the right, and a solution coded in the NetLogo language is shown on the left.

a consequence, it is difficult to assess how well the algorithms are performing at the task i.e. how close they get to the best solution.

In order to gauge better how the algorithms are performing, we tried manually crafting solutions to the Santa Fe Trail problem to see if we could beat the best performing GP and GE solutions as reported in the literature. We also examined several of these solutions, and found that a number of them could be easily improved manually by eliminating unnecessary steps. For example, the solution published in Koza [3] is shown on the left side of Fig. 2 converted from LISP to NetLogo, and a simple manually adjusted variant which eliminates the unnecessary **turn-left turn-right** sequence reduces the number of **move**, **turn-left** or **turn-right** steps taken from 545 down to 405. It is perhaps indicative of some of the limitations of evolutionary algorithms that such a simple improvement was not discovered from the outset, although in any practical application of GP or GE, parameter tuning and manual modification post search is often a possibility to improve the best solutions found.

One GE solution described by Georgiou and Teahan [1] shown in the middle of Fig. 2 reduces the number of steps down to 419. Interestingly, much of the GE solution is similar in structure to the GP solution described by Koza shown on the left of the figure except for **turn-left** actions being replaced with **turn-right** actions. A more recent notably different solution shown to the right of the figure found using GE combined with Novelty Search described by Urbano and Georgiou [7] reduces the number of steps even further down to 331.

Clearly, there is an 'optimal' solution. This consists of just following the path itself—an agent executing just **move**, **turn-left** and **turn-right** operators, and

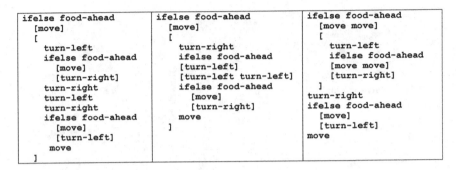

Fig. 2. A GP discovered solution for the Santa Fe Trail Problem published by Koza [3] converted into NetLogo (shown on the left) requiring 545 steps, a GE discovered solution published by Georgiou and Teahan [1] (in the middle) that requires 419 steps and a recent GE with Novelty Search discovered solution published by Urbano and Georgiou [7] (on the right) that reduces the number of steps down to 331.

no conditional food-ahead operators, can follow the path exactly in a minimum number of steps—165. This is significantly smaller than the number of steps taken by the better performing solutions found by GP and GE algorithms, which is typically around 330 to 400 steps.

The optimal solution, however, is overfitted to the problem—it can only work on the Santa Fe Trail itself. The solutions found by GP and GE algorithms on the other hand, although taking a significantly greater number of steps, are more general solutions. We have found that the same solutions do surprisingly well at following completely different trails such as a circle, cross, ring, spiral and square (see the Follow-Trail NetLogo model [6, p. 8]). Surprisingly, the published GP and GE solutions for the Santa Fe Trail problem were found to perform well at following a number of these trails, with a majority of the ants usually ending up completely on the trails, and with only a comparatively small number venturing off trail.

Some results from these experiments are shown in Table 1 which lists results for five different trails (circle, cross, ring, spiral and square—see Fig. 3) for four behaviours: Koza's behaviour that was GP-generated specifically for the Santa Fe Trail (shown on the left of Fig. 2); GE-generated behaviour found by Georgiou and Teahan in 2010 (shown in the middle of Fig. 2); GE-generated behaviour found by Urbano and Georgiou (shown to the right of Fig. 2); and a fourth behaviour as implemented by the NetLogo model that was hand-crafted based on the insights gained from observing the GP and GE-generated behaviours. In these experiments, 1000 turtle agents were created at random locations with random headings at the start of each simulation. They then started executing the same baheviour repeatedly for 1000 ticks after which the percentage of agents on the trail were calculated. 10 runs of each simulation were conducted and results were then averaged.

Table 1. Average percentage of agents that remained on the different shaped trails (as shown in Fig. 3) for the three behaviours shown in Fig. 2 (GP-generated behaviour found by Koza [3], GE-generated behaviour found by Georgiou and Teahan [1] and GE-generated behaviour found by Urbano and Georgiou [7]) and for a manually engineered behaviour ("Look ahead, then left, then right, before moving"). 10 runs were performed in each case. 1000 agents were created at random locations in the environment at the beginning of each run.

Behaviour	Circle	Cross	Ring	Spiral	Square
Koza (1992)	93.2	38.4	63.4	48.5	80.1
Georgiou and Teahan (2010)	99.9	82.9	95.2	65.9	96.6
Urbano and Teahan (2013)	74.4	10.1	13.8	21.8	28.2
Look ahead, then left, then right, before moving	99.8	93.8	97.0	81.4	100.0

Fig. 3. Screenshots of simulations using the five different shaped trails (circle, cross, ring, spiral and square) that were developed for the Follow-Trail NetLogo model [6, p. 8] in order to test out the effectiveness of GP and GE-generated behaviours and compare with manually crafted behaviours.

We can see from the results in Table 1 that Koza's GP-generated behaviour does very well with two of the trails—the circle and the square—but performs poorly with the ring and the spiral trails. Georgiou and Teahan's GE-generated behaviour does well on most of the trails except for the spiral. In contrast, Urbano and Georgiou's GE generated behaviour is the worst performing of all the behaviors despite having the best result on the Santa Fe Trail itself for the three GP or GE-generated behaviours. The manually crafted behaviour that is implemented with the model (which is based on repeatedly performing a sequence of three basic actions—looking ahead, then left, then right—before moving) does well with all trails (100% success for the square trail) with only the spiral trail presenting a problem but still with an 81% success rate. Clearly, GP and GE still has some way to go in order to achieve human-competitive results in this situation. However, the superiority of the manually crafted behaviour is a result of applying general human knowledge. If trained on more than one trail, it is not clear whether GP and GE might develop similar quality solutions and more work needs to be done in this area.

These results do illustrate a useful feature of evolutionary algorithms, however—their ability to find general solutions to a problem rather than generating solutions that are too specific. This also raises the possibility that improved GP and GE solutions found in the future for the Santa Fe Trail problem may in fact simply get better performance by becoming more overfitted to the problem— i.e. they might simply learn to incorporate part of the trail itself by inserting the non-conditional steps that describe the part-trail directly inside their program. Alternatively, they could incorporate a mechanism for coping with some quirk of the trail that does not generalise to other trails. For example, modifying the left solution in Fig. 2 with two move operations instead of one after removing the unnecessary turn-left turn-right sequence results in the number of steps being further reduced down to 365 (see Fig. 1). In order to overcome this danger of overfitting, future experimenters should consider measuring performance against a range of trails, and not just a single trail.

We have also found that an important aspect of the ant's performance, the cost of performing a sensing operation, is not usually being considered when determining how well the ant has performed. Some solutions perform well in relation to the number of motor steps they require, but then perform a significantly greater number of sensing steps in comparison to other solutions. For example, the model in Fig. 1 monitors both motor and sensing steps. For the solution shown, there are 365 motor steps, but there is an additional cost for the ant of 226 sensing steps. The optimal solution, in contrast, requires only 165 motor steps and 0 sensing steps. Again, future experimenters should consider factoring this in their comparisons.

In this paper, we describe our investigations with two specific variations of the Santa Fe Trail problem. The BNF grammars that define the language structure for these variations is shown in Figs. 4 and 5. The grammar labelled BNF-1 in Fig. 4 is similar to the one Georgiou and Teahan [1] used in their GE experiments. This defines a search space semantically equivalent to Koza's original implementation search space. The only difference is that <op> appears before ifelse food-ahead when the <line> non-terminal is defined.

For the second variation using grammar BNF-2 in Fig. 5, no conditional sensing operation (i.e. food-ahead) is allowed, just the motor operations of move, turn-left and turn-right. In this situation, the optimal solution is the only solution, as the trail does not appear to be self-similar where a sequence of motor actions repeated might enable the ant to get through the trail. The purpose of including this grammar in the experiments is to see (for testing purposes) if the new search algorithm can find a solution in a search space where there was only a single known solution which required many steps.

In the next section, we will describe our new search optimisation algorithm that we will then apply to the two variations of the Santa Fe Trail problem (as defined by grammars BNF-1 and BNF-2). It is important to emphasise here that the purpose of the new algorithm was not to find a more effective behaviour for solving the Santa Fe Trail. Instead, the main purpose was to determine if it was possible to generate near-optimal solutions, something that has not been

```
<expr> ::= <line> | <expr> <line>
<line> ::= <op> |
  ifelse food-ahead [<expr>] [<expr>]
<op> ::= turn-left | turn-right | move
```

Fig. 4. BNF-1 grammar definition.

```
<expr> ::= <op> | <expr> <op>
<op> ::= turn-left | turn-right | move
```

Fig. 5. BNF-2 grammar definition.

reported yet in previously published results for the GP and GE algorithms, thereby highlighting possible shortcomings of these algorithms in this respect. (As this was the focus of our investigations, considering multiple trails and factoring in sensing steps as discussed above has been treated as out of scope for this paper, and is therefore left for future investigations.)

3   The New Algorithm

3.1   Design

As with evolutionary programming, we consider the optimisation problem as a search for solutions to a specific task which are represented as programs that are executable in some target programming language. For example, as the programming language with which we wish to implement our design is the agent-oriented programming language NetLogo, then the output of the search are NetLogo programs that can be executed directly in that language without modification (although the algorithm is not restricted to the NetLogo language; it is capable of generating program solutions for any programming language).

When considering the meaning of the terms *agent* and *environment* in this context, we apply a similar meaning adopted by the NetLogo designers [8]. Here agents are software entities that often simulate or model real-world phenomena that follow instructions and move around a (usually) 2D world in the NetLogo environment.

The search optimisation algorithm we have developed to perform the task of solving the Artificial Ant problem (specifically, solving the Santa Fe Trail Problem) has been designed to adhere to the following design principles:

- When a region in the program search space is explored, it should be explored only once and not revisited latter.

- If a particular solution or partial solution is found to be poor, then other solutions that are quantifiably similar should be eliminated from possible future searches.

The idea behind the algorithm is to apply a multi-agent heuristic search optimisation strategy where teams of agents simultaneously search through the program space in parallel. The search problem is characterised using the agent-environment metaphor, where the program space is considered to be an environment which is systematically explored by situated, embodied agents using appropriate behaviours such as hill-climbing and path following, while avoiding as much as possible behaviours such as backtracking and/or crossing back over one's path that incur added costs.

During each iteration, each agent is evaluated based on some problem-specific fitness criteria, and only the fittest are selected to create further child agents that continue the search in the next iteration, with all parent agents being killed off i.e. the population has a fixed upper bound in size at the end of each iteration. At the start of the search (iteration 0), a single parent agent is created which by default performs zero actions. An action is a program instruction as defined by a terminal symbol in the BNF grammar. During an iteration, each child agent continues to expand the search by following a particular path as defined by the grammar. When it encounters a non-terminal symbol, it will create a child agent to search that path. If it encounters a terminal symbol instead, it will add a further action to its behaviour. It does this by maintaining a list of actions it inherits from its parent, and just appends the new action onto the end of the list. There are as many child agents generated as there are possible actions, as determined by the grammar that defines the search problem, in order to ensure the full search space is explored. For example, for the BNF rule defining <op> at the bottom of the BNF-1 grammar, there are three choices consisting of terminals, therefore this would cause three child agents to be created when this rule needed to be expanded.

Once all the rule expansions are completed for a particular agent, a complete program is generated and this is evaluated by running it separately. Two populations of agents are kept: the first for agents that search the program space defined by the grammar that contain partially completed programs defined by their list of actions; and the second for completed programs. The fitness of both types of agents are evaluated each iteration, and those deemed unfit are eliminated from future iterations. Partially completed programs in the first population that are similar to badly performing completed programs in the second population are also eliminated. The overall search is completed according to some termination criteria (e.g. either a solution is found or a maximum number of iterations is exceeded).

The fitness function plays a crucial role in ranking the suitability of the agents' behaviour. This ranking effectively results in a hill-climbing behaviour. Depending on the problem, the fitness function can also be adjusted to take into account other behaviours appropriate for the problem. In the Santa Fe Trail problem, for example, the obvious behaviour to use is hill climbing (where ants that get further down the trail are ranked higher). This can be combined with path following (where ants that go off the trail are assigned a fitness value of 0) and no backtracking (where ants that turn back on themselves are also assigned a fitness value of 0). In the experiments below, fitness is set to the value of the position the ant has moved along the trail if the ant has finished on the trail, with 1 being the value for the start of the trail, and the maximum value being set at the end of the trail. If the agent has not ended up on the trail, then a fitness value of 0 is assigned. In comparison, a standard fitness function used by GP and GE algorithms is simply to count the food eaten. We have also experimented with this fitness function (not reported below), and although this results in solutions being found in various configurations, we have found our hill climbing and path following variant of the fitness function to be more effective for our new algorithm.

The overall design of the search algorithm has incorporated aspects of several search algorithms (breadth-first, best-first, beam, tabu and GE) although it has unique elements which distinguish it from each of those types of searches. As the search tree is being built, sibling nodes are explored in parallel, and therefore the search algorithm explores the search tree like breadth-first search does. However, unlike breadth-first search, the new algorithm is not complete as a heuristic fitness-based approach is used to prune out branches of the tree from being searched. The search algorithm applies a parallel best-first policy to perform the search, where the best performing leaves of the search tree are being searched in parallel in a manner analogous with beam search. As with beam search, the new algorithm generates all successors of nodes at the current level, before moving onto the next level (similar to breadth-first search as well). Also as with beam search, the nodes at the current level are sorted in increasing order of heuristic cost (using the fitness function), and only a fixed number of the best performing nodes (determined by the beam width) are chosen to be expanded. However, unlike beam search, two populations of agents are kept— one with partially completed programs, and one for completed programs which are potential solutions to the problem. This second population maintains the best performing solutions across iterations which clearly distinguishes it from a beam-like search and partially completed programs that are similar to badly performing completed programs are also eliminated. The new search algorithm also has elements that are similar with tabu search, where new partial solutions are created and iteratively updated until some stopping criteria is met. These partial solutions are evaluated by the fitness function to determine which will not be iteratively updated further (these are effectively placed onto a "tabu" list). However, unlike tabu search, the new algorithm in its current implementation does not have any mechanism to revisit these (they are completely eliminated from the search), and again, the two population design clearly distinguishes the new search algorithm from tabu search. Finally, the new search has elements of similarity with GE (which helped to inspire the algorithm) such as a BNF grammar being used to define the programs that are generated during the search and a fitness function being used to rank their performance. However, unlike GE search, the standard genetic operators such as mutation and crossover are not used to vary the search for the new algorithm, and the search does not revisit and/or re-evaluate parts of the search it has already explored.

3.2 An Initial Investigation

As initial proof of concept, we developed a NetLogo model for the Santa Fe Trail using a simplified search for the problem defined by the BNF-2 grammar. We describe the model here as it serves to illustrate important aspects of how the more general search proceeds. This model generates the program actions directly rather than use a separate population of agents to traverse the grammar as for the more general search algorithm described in the next section. The model effectively treats the program search space as a ternary tree that needs to be searched, since for this problem there are just three motor actions to perform and no sensing action. At the start, a single agent is created for the root of the tree. Then for each iteration, each agent creates three child agents before being killed off. The child agents are used to search the three child nodes based on where each agent is located in the tree, and these add the motor action associated with the node (`turn-left`, `turn-right` or `move`) onto their list of actions they have inherited from their parent.

A slider in the interface of the model is used to define the upper bound in the number of active agents used in the search per iteration (this can range from 1 to 50), with poorly performing agents according to the fitness function killed off each iteration. Hence we are able to test out how large a population of agents is needed in order to successfully solve this variation of the Santa-Fe Trail problem. For the fitness function (as discussed in the previous section), the further along the trail the agent has travelled the 'higher' the agent is deemed to be for hill climbing purposes. In addition, any agent that wandered off the trail or doubled back on themselves is killed off.

Table 2 lists some results of running the model. The results shown in the table are for 50 iterations (runs) of the model. If a single agent is kept per iteration, then the average number of motor steps required per solution found is 208.2. This is reduced to close to the optimal number of 165 when more agents are used.

Table 2. Mean number of motor steps (for 50 runs of the model) of solutions found per population size for the simple hill-climbing and path following search algorithm on the Santa Fe Trail problem. (The number of sensing steps is 0 in all cases).

	Population size (i.e. upper bound to the number of agents used per iteration)				
	1	2	3	4	5
Motor steps	208.2	176.3	168.6	166.3	165.6

Clearly, the success of this simplified search algorithm is because the selection of the agents is well-suited to the problem—the agents are killed off if they do not end up on the trail. That is, the problem consists of path following and the agents just employ a form of path following to find the optimal solution. However, the agents do this in an embodied way applying the three motor actions without knowing where the trail is in advance. And arguably, the hill-climbing nature of the algorithm—the use of the fitness function to determine which agents are selected for reproduction—is akin to what happens in evolutionary algorithms such as GP and GE (i.e. evolutionary algorithms rank solutions in the same manner).

We also conducted experiments with GE using the BNF-2 grammar using the jGE-NetLogo extension developed by Georgiou and Teahan [1] to see how GE performs on this variation of the Santa Fe Trail problem. Tellingly, GE was not able to find a solution in any of our runs. The simple algorithm described here, in contrast, always finds a solution, which is invariably the optimal solution if the population size is set at 5 or more, and does this with linear time complexity since there are always a fixed number of agents being created and being kept alive per iteration.

3.3 Grammar-Directed Search

The algorithm discussed in the previous section works on a simplified variation of the Santa Fe Trail which requires a long sequence of terminals (as defined by the <op> non-terminal) to be generated as defined by the BNF-2 grammar. The search problem becomes much more difficult if a more complicated grammar is used such as BNF-1. This involves recursive expressions that reappear as sub-expressions (the <expr> non-terminal, for example). This section describes how the rules of the grammar are expanded as the search proceeds for our more general algorithm whose overall design has been discussed in Sect. 3.1.

The method requires that the grammar is right recursive in order to work more effectively at pruning out branches of the search found to produce poor programs. In the NetLogo model we have developed, when we input the grammar, it is converted into a set of agents representing nodes and links between them as shown in Fig. 6. This is so that the grammar can be more easily visualised in NetLogo and also to simplify the search code. Each non-terminal is represented by rooted trees as shown in the figure. The order that the rule for a non-terminal is loaded determines the order our algorithm will search a possible expansion of a non-terminal.

The pseudo-code for the algorithm is shown in Algorithm 1. The method used by our algorithm is explained in detail as follows. The approach maintains two populations of agents: the first (which we will call *alpha* agents) maintain a set of partially generated programs that are built as a result of the agents traversing in parallel the entire search space of possible programs as determined by the grammar; and the second, a set of agents called *beta* agents that have specifications for completely generated programs and which are tested to see how they perform in the problem. (The terms *alpha* and *beta* used here can be

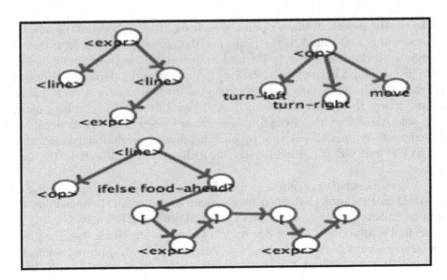

Fig. 6. The grammar BNF-1 represented in NetLogo as a forest of rooted trees using labelled agents for the vertices (e.g. <expr> and move) and unlabelled agents for the directed edges. (Screenshot of the NetLogo model used to implement the new algorithm).

thought of as being analogous to the terms alpha and beta programming used in software engineering). Both populations are updated during each iteration by using a fitness function described in Sect. 3.1 to prune out poorly performing agents. The alpha agents simultaneously traverse the forest of trees defined by the grammar (see lines 6 to 16 in Algorithm 1) while the beta agents which represent fully generated programs (created on line 16) try to traverse the Santa Fe Trail when executed (see line 19).

At the beginning of the search (iteration 0), a single alpha agent is created (line 2) and is positioned at the root node of the tree for the non-terminal that represents the first rule of the grammar. In Fig. 6, this is the tree for <expr> that appears in the top left. There are two possible paths that can be explored at this stage, as there are two links proceeding out of the root node. Hence, two child alpha agents will be generated for these paths and are candidates for keeping into the next iteration. These alpha agents when generated move to the nodes that are linked along the paths. In other words, in iteration 1 of the search, there will be two alpha agents physically located at the two nodes labelled <line> in the top left tree of Fig. 6. If a node represents a non-terminal symbol (its label appears in brackets), then the alpha agent will jump to the root node of the tree for that non-terminal, adding the action to its list of actions. That is, at the end of iteration 1, if these alpha agents are deemed to be fit (see below), there will be two alpha agents sitting at the top of the tree whose root node is labelled <line> (this is the tree at the bottom of the figure). These alpha agents will then continue the search in the same recursive manner, creating child alpha

---

Algorithm 1. Pseudo-code for the grammar-directed search algorithm to solve the Santa Fe Trail problem.

Input: BNF Grammar
Output: Solution for the Santa Fe Problem.

1   *iteration* ← 0
2   create *AlphaAgent* located at root of BNF grammar forest (at the start symbol node)
3   **while** *true* **do**
4   **if** termination criteria is met **then**
5   stop
6   **for** each *AlphaAgent* **do**
7   **if** *CurrentNode* is a terminal node **then**
8   add action to *AlphaAgent*'s list of actions
9   **else**
10   **if** *CurrentNode* does not have zero inward links **then**
11   create new *AlphaAgent* to start traversing grammar for non-terminal
12   terminate *AlphaAgent*
13   **for** each *ChildNode* of *CurrentNode* **do**
14   create new *AlphaAgent* to continue traversing grammar for *ChildNode*
15   **if** reached end of a grammar rule? **then**
16   create new *BetaAgent* using actions from *AlphaAgent*
17   terminate *AlphaAgent*
18   **for** each *BetaAgent* **do**
19   execute the actions associated with this *BetaAgent*
20   determine its *Fitness*
21   **for** each *BetaAgent* with poor *Fitness* value **do**
22   terminate *AlphaAgents* like this *BetaAgent*
23   terminate *BetaAgent*
24   **for** each *AlphaAgent* **do**
25   determine its *Fitness* after rectifying and executing its *Actions*
26   **for** each *AlphaAgent* with poor *Fitness* value **do**
27   terminate *AlphaAgent*
28   *iteration* ← *iteration* + 1

---

agents as needed (inheriting their parent's actions; see line 14), until a leaf node representing a terminal symbol is reached (line 15). At this time, a beta agent with a complete set of actions will be generated (line 16), and then will be evaluated separately from the alpha population (line 20).

As with the beta agent population, a fixed size of alpha agents are maintained each iteration, and only the fittest alpha agents are chosen to continue into the next iteration (lines 26 and 27), and all parent alpha agents die each iteration (lines 12 and 17) since they have already created child agents to continue the search if necessary. This ensures that the design principles outlined in Sect. 3.1 are adhered to. Unlike evolutionary algorithms, the search space is not explored repeatedly. This is possible because we are directly searching the program space in a recursive tree-like manner, and if any branch is deemed to be unfit, the entire sub-branch is eliminated forever from the search. (Note that this sub-branch can be infinite in size).

One question that arises is how to evaluate a set of actions (i.e. program) when it is only partially complete. This is achieved in our model through a process we call *rectification*. (This is performed on line 25). As the set of actions have been generated from a right recursive grammar, one solution is to simply complete the program by adding appropriate fillers that contain no actions. This ensures that when executed, the rectified sets of actions are syntactically correct. For example, a partially complete set of actions may be as follows:

`ifelse food-ahead [move] [ifelse food-ahead [.`

In this case, the else part of the first `ifelse` statement has yet to be expanded, as well as both the then and else parts for the second `ifelse` statement—these are the parts following the unmatched left brackets that need to be filled in. The rectification process simply fills these in with a blank set of instructions (i.e. `ifelse food-ahead [move] [ifelse food-ahead [] []]`), and then this program can be evaluated without any syntax errors.

Note, however, that this simplified method for rectification may lead to viable programs being eliminated from the search (since the unfilled parts of the program may produce an action which is crucial for survival of an agent when it repeats itself in a subsequent iteration by starting over from the beginning again once it has executed all its actions in the previous iteration). An alternative approach would be to only prune out alpha agents for which there are at least one motor action being performed at the beginning of every then and else part of the program. This would then provide the chance for testing the fitness of the partial program (for example, the motor action might result in any agent's program that might be generated in the future to temporarily go off the trail resulting in a fitness ranking of 0). However, this latter technique has not been explored in this paper and is left for future work.

3.4   Results

We have tried out our new algorithm using the two grammars BNF-1 and BNF-2. Unlike the previous algorithm described in Sect. 3.2, the agents that went off the trail or doubled back on themselves were not killed separately, but instead were assigned a value of 0 for the fitness function. The reason for this was to test whether the fitness function could be used as the sole means for ultimately deciding which agents should be pruned. However, the hill-climbing aspects of the fitness function was the same as before—a higher incremental fitness value was assigned to agents that got further down the trail. A separate alpha population was also used to traverse the BNF rule forest as described in the previous section. This was not needed previously as the BNF-2 grammar does not require any sub-expressions to be expanded.

The interface of our NetLogo model allows us to set parameters that specify the upper bounds in the size of the alpha and beta agent populations at the end of each iteration, and monitors also report various details such as the number of iterations, the number of alpha and beta agents used and the number of steps of each solution. Table 3 presents selected results for different alpha and beta population sizes (represented by the α and β columns respectively). The "Average steps" column provides the average number of motor steps found by the solutions (averaged across 5 runs). The "% solved" column lists the percentage of runs that found a solution.

Table 3. Selected results on variations of the Santa Fe Trail problem for the BNF-1 and BNF-2 grammars when using the NetLogo model that implements our new algorithm. α is the upper bound in size used for the alpha population; β is the upper bound in size used for the beta population; and I is the number of iterations required. The results are averaged across five runs. † indicates no value was recorded if there were no solutions found by the algorithm for the specified parameters after 2000 iterations.

α	β	I	Alpha agents used	Beta agents used	Average steps	% solved
For the problem defined by the BNF-1 grammar:						
100	10	1154	150747	2048	165	100%
100	5	1154	150884	1988	165	100%
100	1	1184	153858	1447	165	100%
50	10	1162	76042	1168	165	100%
20	20	†	†	†	†	0%
10	10	†	†	†	†	0%
For the problem defined by the BNF-2 grammar:						
20	5	824.0	12072	1624.2	165.0	100%
10	5	860.0	8679.4	858.8	172.0	100%
1..5	5	2000	†	†	†	0%
1	1..n	2000	†	†	†	0%
20	2	2000	†	†	†	0%
10	2	881.5	5693.5	856	176.5	20%
1..5	2	2000	†	†	†	0%
1..n	1	2000	†	†	†	0%

The results show that when the alpha population is sufficiently large for the problem, the search algorithm is able to find an optimal or near optimal solution (165 motor steps and either 0 or 1 sensor steps). For example, a run for the BNF-1 grammar problem with $\alpha = 100$ and $\beta = 1$ was able to find a near optimal solution, but it included one `ifelse food-ahead` statement. It generated the following commands:

```
move move move turn-right move move move move move ...
turn-left move move ifelse food-ahead [move ...
```
(152 intervening move | turn-left | turn-right commands that replicate the intervening trail exactly) ...
```
turn-left move][move].
```

This solution works because the ifelse food-ahead statement has no effect: when it is executed, there is food ahead on the trail, so the else part will never get executed, and the then part continues with commands to follow the trail exactly.

One solution found by a run with $\alpha = 50$ and $\beta = 10$ also included one ifelse food-ahead statement:

```
move move move ifelse food-ahead [turn-left][turn-right ...
```
(159 intervening move | turn-left | turn-right commands that replicate the intervening trail exactly) ...
```
turn-left move].
```

This time the then part of the ifelse statement has no effect since there is no food when it is executed.

This illustrates that the algorithm is exploring a much larger search space for the BNF-1 problem, and successfully finding alternative solutions even though heavily biased by the fitness function to closely follow the trail (and therefore more likely to generate the optimal solution).

The model can also output the actions of agents that have been generated at intermediate stages of the search, and various superfluous conditional constructions were also observed such as:

```
ifelse food-ahead [ move ] [ move ].
```

The execution time for our algorithm varies depending on the setting chosen for the interface speed slider, and on what display options are chosen for the model since the actions of the agents can be seen being executed in the environment as the model is run. When the speed slider is set to the fastest setting, and update of the display is turned off, then a run for the BNF-2 grammar typically takes from 5 to 10 min to perform on a MacBook Pro 2.4 Ghz Inter Core 2 Duo processor with 4 Gb RAM (but this varies greatly according to the α and β parameters used). In contrast, a run for the BNF-1 grammar can take much longer due to the considerably larger search space. The run when $\alpha = 100$ and $\beta = 10$, for example, typically took over 40 min processing time. The values for 'Alpha agents used' and 'Beta agents used' shown in Table 3 give a better indication of the space and time complexities for the algorithm since this reflects how many alternative alpha and beta agents were required to be created, evaluated and subsequently killed, during the run.

In comparison, the best previously published results in the GP/GE literature are the solution discovered by Urbano and Georgiou [7] shown to the right of Fig. 2 which requires 331 steps, and a solution discovered by Headle-and and Teahan [2] requiring just 303 steps via population seeding of GE using Grammatical Herding. These are still well short of the 165 steps in the optimal solution. However, it is unclear whether GP and GE would be able to find the optimal solution if given similar resources to our new algorithm (such as a heavily biased fitness function) and this comparison is left for future work.

4   Conclusion

A new grammar directed heuristic search optimisation algorithm for automatically generating programming solutions to variations of the Santa Fe Trail Artificial Ant problem has been discussed. The new algorithm uses two populations of agents to search the program space (one population for partially completed programs and a second population for fully completed programs, both with a fixed upper bound in population size which is set at the start of the search). The main purpose of the new algorithm was to see if we could devise a method to generate optimal solutions for the Santa Fe Trail problem, something that Genetic Programming (GP) and Grammatical Evolution (GE) algorithms have yet to achieve. Experimental results show that the algorithm is able to find an optimal solution 100% of the time using various modest fixed population sizes. For example, the least number of resources used (in terms of agents created by the algorithm) was found to occur when the upper bound in population size for partially completed programs was 50 and the upper bound in population size for fully completed programs was 10.

Path following and hill climbing behaviour were used to find the optimal solution. For other problems, the use of other behaviours may be more appropriate; for example, when searching mazes where the location of the optimal path can not be so clearly distinguished in advance, hill climbing behaviour is problematical, and an alternative behaviour such as wall following might be better suited to the problem.

Two main design principles for the new algorithm were adhered to in order to overcome known inadequacies of evolutionary search: firstly, a region in the search space is explored only once by the algorithm and is not revisited latter; and secondly, if a particular solution or partial solution is found to be poor, then the algorithm eliminates other solutions that are quantifiably similar from possible future searches.

The process of rectification (which requires modifying a partially complete program so that it can be tested for fitness) is crucial to the overall success of the new algorithm. If we can successfully manage to prune out unfit sub-branches of the search, this will reduce the search cost substantially. Due to the structured nature of our search algorithm, we have control over which parts of the search space are searched and which are not. However, at the same time, we need to be very careful which sub-branches can be legitimately pruned away. This problem is an area we are actively investigating.

The way the agents' actions are repeated needs further work. At the moment, an agent which survives into the next iteration will automatically have its actions repeated, which for an artificial ant problem will result in the agent repeating the path it took, but from where it ended last time, not from the origin. If the agent then survives the next iteration, it will continue to have its actions repeated. This method of handling repetition may not be the best policy, and also requires further investigation.

References

1. Georgiou, L., Teahan, W.J.: Grammatical evolution and the Santa Fe Trail Problem. In: Proceedings of the International Conference on Evolutionary Computation (ICEC 2010), Valencia, Spain, pp. 10–19 (2010)
2. Headleand, C., Teahan, W.J.: Swarm based population seeding of grammatical evolution. Comput. Sci. Syst. Biol. **6**, 132–135 (2013)
3. Koza, J.R.: Genetic Programming: On the Programming of Computers by Means of Natural Selection. MIT Press, Cambridge (1992)
4. Koza, J.R., Keane, M.A., Streeter, M.J., Mydlowec, W., Yu, J., Lanza, G.: Genetic Programming IV: Routine Human-Competitive Machine Intelligence (v. 4). Springer, Heidelberg (2003)
5. O'Neill, M., Ryan, C.: Grammatical evolution. IEEE Trans. Evol. Comput. **5**(4), 349–358 (2001)
6. Teahan, W.J.: Artificial Intelligence: Exercises I-Agents and Environments. Ventus Publishing Aps, Denmark (2010)
7. Urbano, P., Georgiou, L.: Improving grammatical evolution in Santa Fe Trail using novelty search. In: Proceedings of the European Conference on Artificial Life (ECAL 2013), Taormina, Italy, pp. 917–924 (2013)
8. Wilensky, U.: NetLogo. Center for Connected Learning and Computer-Based Modeling, Northwestern University, Evanston, IL (1999). http://ccl.northwestern.edu/netlogo/

Synergies Between Reinforcement Learning and Evolutionary Dynamic Optimisation

Aman Soni[✉]ⓘ, Peter R. Lewis, and Anikó Ekárt

Aston Labs for Intelligent Collectives Engineering (ALICE),
Aston University, Birmingham, UK
sonia2@aston.ac.uk
http://alice.aston.ac.uk

Abstract. A connection has recently been drawn between dynamic optimization and reinforcement learning problems as subsets of a broader class of sequential decision-making problems. We present a unified approach that enables the cross-pollination of ideas between established communities, and could help to develop rigorous methods for algorithm comparison and selection for real-world resource-constrained problems.

1 Introduction

Decision problems are often encountered in system design and control. If the underlying environment changes, the problem is dynamic and requires new decisions over time. There is a need for robust problem-independent search algorithms in cases where knowledge of optimization function can only be gained through sampling, or if there are insufficient resources to construct a problem-dependent algorithm [1]. Current approaches to construct problem-independent algorithms are to frame the problem as a Dynamic Optimisation Problem (DOP) [2] or as a Reinforcement Learning Problem (RLP) [3].

DOPs, often tackled using Evolutionary Dynamic Optimisation (EDO) algorithms, are usually seen as tracking moving optima problems [2]. On the other hand, RLPs are often defined as Markov Decision Processes (MDPs) [3]. Fu et al. [4] proposed Sequential Decision-Making Problems (SDMPs) as a class of problem that includes DOPs and RLPs. This is useful as EDO and RL algorithms specialise in different types of SDMPs [5] and the SDMP perspective creates an opportunity to cross-pollinate ideas across well-established research.

To realise this opportunity, SDMP definitions should include sufficient information for EDO and RL algorithms to be substituted or hybridised. This creates a need for methods to compare performance across EDO and RL algorithms. To understand how an algorithm will perform on real-world problems with limited resources, comparisons should be made under varying resource constraints. These comparisons can be used to create a rigorous method for algorithm selection. There may be further applications for meta-heuristics at run-time.

© Springer International Publishing AG, part of Springer Nature 2018
P. R. Lewis et al. (Eds.): ALIA 2016, CCIS 732, pp. 91–96, 2018.
https://doi.org/10.1007/978-3-319-90418-4_7

This research has immediate applicability to challenging real world problems in domains of robotics [6], space [7], vehicle routing [8], traffic control [9], image recognition [10], inventory management [11] and game play [12].

2   DOPs Versus RLPs

Based on Fu et al. [4], we define a DOP as: *Given an optimization problem F, an optimization algorithm G to solve F, and an optimization period $[t_0, t_e]$, F is a DOP if during $[t_0, t_e]$ the underlying fitness landscape changes and G has to react by providing new solutions where E calculates the estimated reward at each time step.* In contrast to Fu et al. [4] we consider fitness function f to be static. When the state of the environment at time t is a set of variables s_t, and the action taken at time t is a_t, a DOP can be defined[1] as:

$$max \sum_{t=0}^{t_e} E(f(s_t, a_t)). \tag{1}$$

Sutton and Barto [3] define the general form of the RLP as a problem where an agent, for a sequence of discrete time steps, t, at each t evaluates its representation of the environment's state, $s_t \in \mathbb{S}$, where $\mathbb{S}$ is the set of all possible states, and selects an action to perform, $a_t \in \mathbb{A}(s_t)$, where $\mathbb{A}(s_t)$ is the set of available actions for the state s_t. As a consequence of the action, a_t, the environment moves to a new state, s_{t+1} and provides a numerical reward to the agent for the next time step, $r_{t+1} \in \mathbb{R}$. The agent builds a *policy* π for each t, where $\pi_t(s, a)$ is the probability that the selected action $a_t = a$ if $s_t = s$. The solution is a policy π that maximises[2] the total sum of expected rewards. If r denotes the reward function, an RLP can be defined as:

$$\sum_{t=0}^{t_e} r(\arg \max[\pi_t(s_t, a_t)], s_t). \tag{2}$$

The similarities between the definitions of DOP (1) and RLP (2) are striking and support the view that DOPs and RLPs are subsets of a broader class of SDMPs [4]. In both definitions the reward (or fitness) returned is determined by the effects of an action on the current state of the environment. Each problem seeks to maximise the accumulated sum of the returned value and algorithm performance is determined by the values accumulated over the interval $[t_0, t_e]$.

Two significant differences relate to time-linkage between states. The first is that DOP (1) accumulates the maximum reward at every t while RLP (2) maximises the accumulated sum of discounted future rewards. The second difference is that the state representation in DOP (1) is a part of the problem specification while RLP (2) tracks the received rewards using state-action pairs (s_t, a_t) in the

---

[1] Notation has been adjusted to aid comparison to RLP (2).
[2] Maximization problems are considered without a loss of generality.

learning policy π. This implies that DOP (1) does not cater for time-linkage between states, while the policy π in RLP (2) tracks state transitions.

Another similarity is, EDO algorithms compare individuals in a population set, while RL algorithms select from a policy-value set. These actions occur at every at time step.

3   Towards a Unified Approach

EDO algorithms assume a fitness function [4], and typically use an offline environment before the solution is applied to the problem instance [13]. On the other hand, RL algorithms assume some observability of state and a reward function [3]. A unified approach can provide guidance so that current tacit community knowledge is made explicit in problem definition. This makes synthetic and real-world problems available to both EDO and RL algorithms.

RL algorithms can learn online under dynamic conditions without a need for an *a priori* model or simulator [3]. This is a major benefit when the model is unknown or too complex to simulate accurately [6]. Additionally, RL algorithms exploit time-linkage between states, making convergence to an optima quicker if this information is available [3]. However, RL algorithms are considered both slow and resource intensive [14]. On the other hand, EDO algorithms need only evolve policies that directly map states to actions, a major advantage in problems with large or continuous action spaces [15]. EA policies need only specify an action for each state, which can be simpler to represent than learning methods that specify the value of each state-action pair [15]. Suitable policy representations can be evolved rather than needing to be design beforehand [14]. When state information is uncertain, it may be advantageous to use EDO algorithms [6].

Figure 1 shows the unified problem definition space, typical algorithms that overlap, and corresponding gaps in both problems and algorithms. A unified approach provides further opportunities to develop new algorithms, based on the strengths of both EDO and RL, to add to the work that currently spans these research communities.

In this section we present four key open research questions that we see as necessary to realise in order to gain the benefits of a unified SDMP framework.

What are the overarching dimensions of the SDMP space? We propose an approach that divides characteristics of SDMPs into two high-level categories, namely the environment state information and the dynamics of the environment. Environment state information would define SDMP dimensions for the number, range and type of state variables. The dynamics on the environment include the degree [17], rate and pattern of change [2] along with affect of time-linkage between states [3] and certainty in sensing and state transition prediction [6]. Positioning of problem instances in the SDMP space will then be determined by dynamics of the environment state, the size of the state-action space, and the effect of time-linkage between states.

There is a need for configurable synthetic problems that provide good coverage of the SDMP definition space (Fig. 1) to test algorithm performance on

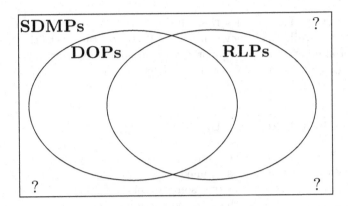

Fig. 1. Unified sequential decision-making problem definition space with corresponding typical algorithms and techniques. Source [16].

different dimension-value combinations. For some problems, dimension values may be static for the instance, while for others they may change.

How should we measure algorithm performance? The solution requirements have a determining role in measuring algorithm performance. Navigation problems require an always available solution, although it can change during navigation, while a manufacturing robot requires control systems with a high level of precision that should not change during operation. Collision avoidance requires real-time responses in a potentially rapidly changing environment. Whether an optimum is known, and the desired minimum solution quality with respect to the optimum, should be considered for algorithm selection and required training, or for bounding algorithm run-times. Other considerations are certainty of time between decision points and whether the relationship of the current state to the life-time of the problem is known.

We argue that it is that we can only *meaningfully compare algorithm in terms of the solution requirements.*

When can we compare performance across algorithms? Measures, such as generations-to-convergence or best-of- generation are used to compare population-based EDO algorithms [15] and do not allow for comparison to non-population-based algorithms [18]. EDO algorithms currently ignore simulation time [4] for performance measures. Furthermore it is not clear how the solution is applied to the environment [2,4]. While many RL algorithms operate online, there are cases where prior knowledge is gained from training [19], or updates to the learning policy are delegated [6]. *SDMPs require methods to compare the online performance of algorithms.*

How do resource constraints effect algorithm performance? In the real world, resources including sensors, memory, power and time are limited. Recent work in this area aims to reduce resource usage [20], or for algorithms to learn to reduce the computational resource and runtime [21]. There is a range of techniques to analyse algorithm time complexity [1] or build models of the run-time [22] that can help gain an understanding of how resource constraints effect solution quality. Use of these techniques could *help design effective algorithms for cases that require specific resources (e.g. battery life) to be conserved.*

A Rigorous Method for Algorithm Selection. In practice, there is a necessary trade-off between performance, solution quality and resource usage. Some considerations for algorithm selection include where the algorithm performs well with high-dimensional and continuous states, or if it is know that an algorithm copes well with change in the environment state dynamics. Experimental work on methods to estimate algorithm performance under constrained resources should be measured against the solution requirements.

This research will allow us to gather information to *develop a rigorous method for algorithm selection.* A further application could be to run-time meta-heuristics.

4 Conclusions

We have presented a unifying perspective of RLPs and DOPs as SDMPs. We have argued that a unified SDMP framework allows for the cross-pollination of ideas between well establish research communities. The SDMP framework will be supported by configurable synthetic problems that can model constrained resources, as is the case in the real world.

We proposed the mapping of problems in the SDMP space. This requires both theoretical and experimental research on algorithm performance. The performance should be measured against the solution requirements, over varying resource constraints.

This work would help develop a rigorous method for algorithm selection balanced between solution quality, algorithm efficiency and resource usage. By framing the selection method as an SDMP, this research has potential application to run-time meta-heuristics.

References

1. Oliveto, P.S., He, J., Yao, X.: Time complexity of evolutionary algorithms for combinatorial optimization: a decade of results. Int. J. Autom. Comput. **4**(3), 281–293 (2007)
2. Nguyen, T., Yang, S., Branke, J.: Evolutionary dynamic optimization: a survey of the state of the art. Swarm Evol. Comput. **6**, 1–24 (2012)
3. Sutton, R.S., Barto, A.G.: Reinforcement Learning: An Introduction, vol. 1. MIT press, Cambridge (1998)
4. Fu, H., Lewis, P.R., Sendhoff, B., Tang, K., Yao, X.: What are dynamic optimization problems? In: IEEE Congress on Evolutionary Computing (CEC), pp. 1550–1557 (2014)

5. Fu, H., Lewis, P.R., Yao, X.: A Q-learning based evolutionary algorithm for sequential decision making problems. In: Parallel Problem Solving from Nature (PPSN). VUB AI Lab (2014)
6. Wiering, M., van Otterlo, M.: Reinforcement Learning: State-of-the-Art, vol. 12. Springer, Heidelberg (2012). https://doi.org/10.1007/978-3-642-27645-3
7. Myers, P.L., Spencer, D.B.: Application of a multi-objective evolutionary algorithm to the spacecraft stationkeeping problem. Acta Astronautica **127**, 76–86 (2016)
8. Tan, K.C., Cheong, C.Y., Goh, C.K.: Solving multiobjective vehicle routing problem with stochastic demand via evolutionary computation. Eur. J. Oper. Res. **177**(2), 813–839 (2007)
9. Münst, W., Dannheim, C., Gay, N., Malnar, B., Al-mamun, M., Icking, C., Hagen, F.: Managing intersections in the cloud, pp. 329–334 (2015)
10. Fergus, R., Fei-Fei, L., Perona, P., Zisserman, A.: Learning object categories from Google's image search. In: Tenth IEEE International Conference on Computer Vision, ICCV 2005, vol. 2, pp. 1816–1823. IEEE (2005)
11. Laumanns, M., Thiele, L., Deb, K., Zitzler, E.: Combining convergence and diversity in evolutionary multiobjective optimization. Evol. Comput. **10**(3), 263–282 (2002)
12. Silver, D., Huang, A., Maddison, C.J., Guez, A., Sifre, L., van den Driessche, G., Schrittwieser, J., Antonoglou, I., Panneershelvam, V., Lanctot, M., Dieleman, S., Grewe, D., Nham, J., Kalchbrenner, N., Sutskever, I., Lillicrap, T., Leach, M., Kavukcuoglu, K., Graepel, T., Hassabis, D.: Mastering the game of Go with deep neural networks and tree search. Nature **529**(7587), 484–489 (2016)
13. Jin, Y.J.Y., Branke, J.: Evolutionary optimization in uncertain environments-a survey. IEEE Trans. Evol. Comput. **9**(3), 303–317 (2005)
14. Drugan, M.M.: Synergies between evolutionary algorithms and reinforcement learning. In: Proceedings of the Companion Publication of the 2015 Annual Conference on Genetic and Evolutionary Computation, GECCO Companion 2015, pp. 723–740. ACM (2015)
15. Eiben, A.E., Schoenauer, M.: Evolutionary computing. Inf. Process. Lett. **82**(1), 1–6 (2002)
16. Soni, A., Lewis, P.R., Ekárt, A.: Offline and online time in sequential decision-making problems. In: IEEE CIDUE. IEEE Press (2016)
17. Uzor, C.J., Gongora, M., Coupland, S., Passow, B.N.: Real-world dynamic optimization using an adaptive-mutation compact genetic algorithm. In: 2014 IEEE Symposium on Computational Intelligence in Dynamic and Uncertain Environments (CIDUE), pp. 17–23. IEEE (2014)
18. Cruz, C., González, J.R., Pelta, D.A.: Optimization in dynamic environments: a survey on problems, methods and measures. Soft Comput. **15**(7), 1427–1448 (2011)
19. Dearden, R., Friedman, N., Andre, D.: Model based Bayesian exploration. In: Proceedings of the Fifteenth Conference on Uncertainty in Artificial Intelligence, pp. 150–159. Morgan Kaufmann Publishers Inc. (1999)
20. Piatkowski, N., Lee, S., Morik, K.: Integer undirected graphical models for resource-constrained systems. Neurocomputing **173**, 9–23 (2016)
21. Graves, A.: Adaptive computation time for recurrent neural networks. arXiv preprint arXiv:1603.08983 (2016)
22. Hutter, F., Xu, L., Hoos, H.H., Leyton-Brown, K.: Algorithm runtime prediction: methods & evaluation. In: International Joint Conference on Artificial Intelligence (IJCAI), pp. 4197–4201, January 2015

Improving the Effectiveness of Genetic Programming Using Continuous Self-adaptation

Thomas D. Griffiths[✉] and Anikó Ekárt

Aston Lab for Intelligent Collectives Engineering (ALICE), Aston University,
Aston Triangle, Birmingham B4 7ET, UK
{grifftd1,a.ekart}@aston.ac.uk

Abstract. Genetic Programming (GP) is a form of nature-inspired computing, introduced over 30 years ago, with notable success in problems such as symbolic regression. However, there remains a lot of relatively unexploited potential for solving hard, real-world problems. There is consensus in the GP community that the lack of effective real-world benchmark problems negatively impacts the quality of research [4]. When a GP system is initialised, a number of parameters must be provided. The optimal setup configuration is often not known, due to the fact that many of the values are problem and domain specific, meaning the GP system is unable to produce satisfactory results. We believe that the implementation of continuous self-adaptation, along with the introduction of tunable and suitably difficult benchmark problems, will allow for the creation of more robust GP systems that are resilient to failure.

Keywords: Genetic Programming · Self-adaptation · Benchmarks
Tartarus

1 An Introduction to Genetic Programming

Nature-inspired evolutionary computing methods model natural processes and phenomena, in order to develop novel problem solving techniques. GP draws inspiration from the Darwinian evolution paradigm, based on the theory that populations evolve and are improved through small incremental changes over time. These small changes increase an individual's ability to compete, survive and reproduce, leading onto the main tenet of evolution; *survival of the fittest* [1].

A GP system contains a pool of individual candidate solutions, known as the population. These individuals are responsible for creating solutions to the problem being attempted. During the run of a GP system, multiple iterations, known as generations, are executed and analysed. Each generation consists of three distinct stages: Selection, Recombination and Mutation. After this, the performance of the solutions is assessed using a *fitness function*. Each individual in the population is assigned a fitness score based on the performance of the

© Springer International Publishing AG, part of Springer Nature 2018
P. R. Lewis et al. (Eds.): ALIA 2016, CCIS 732, pp. 97–102, 2018.
https://doi.org/10.1007/978-3-319-90418-4_8

solution they generated, an example GP system is illustrated in Fig. 1. These processes are repeated until a suitable solution is generated, or another termination criterion is reached.

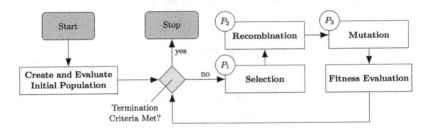

Fig. 1. The stages of a GP system

2   Initialising a GP System

GP has proven to be an effective technique; however, it is often hard to correctly set up and initialise the system. This is due to the fact that the system utilises many different parameters, the values of which vary depending on the domain of the problem and the environment. Failure to set appropriate initialisation parameters often leads to the GP system being unable to generate satisfactory solutions. This failure may be attributed to GP being unable to solve the problem, when in reality, it may be due to unsuitable initialisation parameter values. We believe that this difficulty in initialisation creates a significant barrier to usage and may be partly responsible for the slow uptake of GP in other fields of research. In order to combat this we propose the creation of a GP framework, which will utilise elements of self-adaptation to improve parameter initialisation.

The proposed GP framework will be designed in accordance with the proposed basic requirements of an Open-Ended Evolution (OEE) system [2]. Many evolutionary systems currently in use, lack many of the characteristics present in biological systems, and more crucially, they commonly suffer from premature convergence to a sub-optimal solution. In the majority of cases, once an evolutionary system has converged to some quasi-stable state, nothing fundamentally new will occur. Conversely, an OEE system is designed to be capable of continually producing a stream of novel and different solutions.

3   Benchmark Problems

It has been said that GP has a 'toy problem problem' [3], and that many of the benchmarks used in the field of GP are trivially simple. There has been discussion within the GP community regarding the need to develop a suite of new benchmark tests [4]. One important aspect when creating a benchmark is identifying the desirable characteristics of a problem. One of the key characteristics

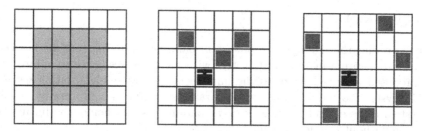

(a) Valid start positions   (b) Example start position   (c) Example final position

Fig. 2. Tartarus problem examples

of a benchmark is for the problem to have *tunable difficulty* [4]. This is where multiple instances of the same problem can be created in a controlled manner, allowing for testing to be conducted under increasingly difficult circumstances.

We propose that the Tartarus problem (TP), with a few minor modifications, could be a suitable benchmark problem candidate. Originally introduced by Teller [5], TP is a relatively simple, grid-based exploratory problem. An agent, with a finite number of moves, and a number of moveable blocks are placed in a $n \times n$ environment. They are randomly placed within the central area of size $(n-2) \times (n-2)$, as shown by the shaded grid-squares in Fig. 2a. The goal of the agent is to create a strategy, which is able locate the blocks and push them to the edge of the environment. The canonical TP instance consists of a 6×6 grid, with six blocks and a single agent with 80 moves, an example instance start and finish positions are shown in Fig. 2b and c respectively.

As both the agent and the blocks are randomly placed, and the orientation of the agent is randomly assigned, at the start of an instance the agent has no knowledge of its own location, or the location of the blocks. At all times the agent is able to see any objects in the 8 grid-squares surrounding it. The agent can attempt to push blocks directly in front of itself, but is only successful if the space the block is being pushed into is empty. The agent is able to execute three actions: move forward F, turn left L and turn right R. An example sequence of actions is outlined in Fig. 3.

$F \rightarrow F \rightarrow L \rightarrow F \rightarrow L \rightarrow F \rightarrow F \rightarrow F \rightarrow R \rightarrow R \rightarrow F \rightarrow F \rightarrow R \rightarrow F \rightarrow F \rightarrow F \rightarrow L \dots$

$\dots F \rightarrow L \rightarrow L \rightarrow F \rightarrow F \rightarrow R \rightarrow F \rightarrow L \rightarrow F \rightarrow L \rightarrow F \rightarrow L \rightarrow F \rightarrow L \rightarrow F \rightarrow F \rightarrow R$

Fig. 3. Sequence of actions taken by an agent

In previous work we have shown that it is possible to tune the difficulty of a TP instances in a predictable manner [6]. This tuning of difficulty is achieved through the alteration of the grid-size, the number of blocks present in the TP instance, and the number of moves available to the agent. These changes in parameter values, when combined, lead to a controlled and measurable change in instance difficulty.

4   Self-adaptation

We believe that the modification of system parameters during runtime has the potential to create a more robust system with increased resilience to failure [7]. The proposed approach involves the implementation of self-adaptation within the GP system to modify the system parameters. This is a process by which the system assesses and modifies its own parameters autonomously during its execution without the need for human input.

Self-adaptation has been used previously in GP [8], however, in these implementations the self-adaptation was triggered at discrete preset intervals, usually at every generations. One of the drawbacks of this approach is the fact that the self-adaptation is triggered by external factors, rather than by internal factors, and therefore the performance or progress of the system is not considered. We propose a new approach in which the program is assessed on a continuous basis and the self-adaptation is triggered by solution progress and problem instance knowledge. This allows for the self-adaptation to be triggered when deemed necessary, rather than at discrete preset intervals as done previously.

The self-adaptation being introduced into the GP system will run concurrently alongside the existing evolutionary processes, as shown in Fig. 4. The continuous progress assessment is able to trigger the self-adaptation at any stage in the generation and make changes at runtime. It is possible that the self-adaptation will not be triggered during the execution of a particular generation, giving the system the ability to chose when to trigger the self-adaptation. This allows for a more robust and flexible process to be created, leading to the evolution of a system which is more resilient to premature convergence and failure.

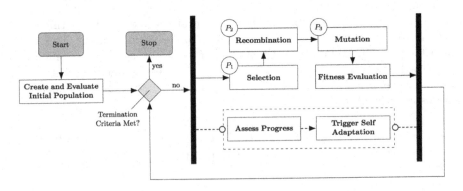

Fig. 4. Introduction of self-adaptation in GP

Our envisaged self-adaptation will build on state of the art in adaptive operators and parameter tuning, such as the recent work by Kalkreuth et al. [9]. The novelty of our approach lies in the fact that it will address the global generation level rather than the operator level.

5   Research Approach and Methodology

The research will be conducted using an empirical approach. This approach relies on the formulation of hypotheses, which can be tested and conclusions drawn. The hypotheses are either falsified or corroborated by the results of experiments carried out in the course of the research. It is for this reason that the first contribution, the Tartarus problem benchmark, has been realised first. The benchmark will be used to test the improved GP system, providing data which will be used to test the remaining research hypotheses.

The initial hypotheses are:

1. It is possible to successfully parameterise a GP system, by incorporating self-adaptation into the evolutionary process to produce suitable system parameter values.
   By doing so, the pressure to initialise parameters suitably to the problem at hand is reduced as the parameters self-adapt throughout the run to facilitate generation of satisfactory solutions.
2. Self-adaptation can be used at runtime to assist in preventing premature convergence and help maintain a suitable level of diversity in the population.
   Through self-adaptation exploration and exploitation will take place automatically, without the need for human intervention, as and when needed.
3. Allowing the self-adaptation to be triggered when it is deemed necessary by the system will provide a greater benefit than the current method of triggering at discrete intervals.

6   Conclusion

It is believed that the redesigned process of triggering self-adaptation at runtime will provide benefits in both the success of the overall GP system and the performance of the solutions generated. In addition to this, the system parameter self-adaptation instead of the need for suitable initialisation will help prevent premature convergence. This is believed to be one of the major stumbling blocks preventing the widespread usage of GP, therefore we propose to make GP more accessible to practitioners in fields outside of computer science. A combination of the improved self-adaptation and accessibility, coupled with the improved benchmarks, should enable GP related research to progress effectively.

References

1. Koza, J.R.: Genetic Programming: On the Programming of Computers by Means of Natural Selection. MIT Press, Cambridge (1992)
2. Taylor, T.: Requirements for open-ended evolution in natural and artificial systems. In: EvoEvo Workshop at the 13th European Conference on Artificial Life, ECAL 2015 (2015)

3. McDermott, J., White, D.R., Luke, S., Manzoni, L., Castelli, M., Vanneschi, L., Jaskowski, W., Krawiec, K., Harper, R., De Jong, K., O'Reilly, U.M.: Genetic programming needs better benchmarks. In: Soule, T., et al. (eds.) Proceedings of the 14th International Conference on Genetic and Evolutionary Computation, GECCO 2012, pp. 791–798 (2012)

4. White, D.R., McDermott, J., Castelli, M., Manzoni, L., Goldman, B.W., Kronberger, G., Jaśkowski, W., O'Reilly, U.M., Luke, S.: Better GP benchmarks: community survey results and proposals. Genet. Program. Evolvable Mach. 14(1), 3–29 (2013)

5. Teller, A.: The evolution of mental models. In: Advances in Genetic Programming, pp. 199–217 (1994)

6. Griffiths, T.D., Ekárt, A.: Improving the Tartarus problem as a benchmark in genetic programming. In: McDermott, J., Castelli, M., Sekanina, L., Haasdijk, E., García-Sánchez, P. (eds.) EuroGP 2017. LNCS, vol. 10196, pp. 278–293. Springer, Cham (2017). https://doi.org/10.1007/978-3-319-55696-3_18

7. Eiben, A.E., Hinterding, R., Michalewicz, Z.: Parameter control in evolutionary algorithms. IEEE Trans. Evol. Comput. 3(2), 124–141 (1999)

8. Harding, S., Miller, J., Banzhaf, W.: Developments in Cartesian genetic programming: self-modifying CGP. Genet. Program Evolvable Mach. 11(3–4), 397–439 (2010)

9. Kalkreuth, R., Rudolph, G., Krone, J.: Improving convergence in Cartesian genetic programming using adaptive crossover, mutation and selection. In: 2015 IEEE Symposium Series on Computational Intelligence, pp. 1415–1422 (2015)

Human-Like Systems

Capturing Human Intelligence for Modelling Cognitive-Based Clinical Decision Support Agents

Ali Rezaei-Yazdi$^{(\boxtimes)}$ and Christopher D. Buckingham

Aston University, Aston Triangle, Birmingham B4 7ET, UK
a.rezaei-yazdi@aston.ac.uk

Abstract. The success of intelligent agents in clinical care depends on the degree to which they represent and work with human decision makers. This is particularly important in the domain of clinical risk assessment where such agents either conduct the task of risk evaluation or support human clinicians with the task. This paper provides insights into how to understand and capture the cognitive processes used by clinicians when collecting the most important data about a person's risks. It attempts to create some theoretical foundations for developing clinically justifiable and reliable decision support systems for initial risk screening. The idea is to direct an assessor to the most informative next question depending on what has already been asked using a mixture of probabilities and heuristics. The method was tested on anonymous mental health data collected by the GRiST risk and safety tool (www.egrist.org).

Keywords: Intelligent agents · Clinical intelligence
Clinical Decision Support Systems · Dynamic data collection
Risk assessment · Healthcare · eHealth

1 Introduction

Successful intelligent agents are those which can learn and utilise human expertise. This is of particular importance in the health-care sector where computerised systems aim to facilitate important clinical tasks including risk assessment [1,2]. For mental health, evaluating risks such as suicide and self-harm is particularly challenging, because the symptoms, motives and deterrents are often abstract and difficult to measure. Here, intelligent agents such as certain types of Clinical Decision Support Systems (CDSSs) can play an important role by guiding users towards the most informative data features and advising on the risks associated with the collected data. If they are to be used in real-world settings, it is crucial that these computer agents are completely reliable.

Although recent reviews on the impact of CDSSs on the quality of healthcare have suggested an overall improvement [3,4], difficulties remain with modelling

This work was part funded by the EIT Health GRaCE-AGE project.

P. R. Lewis et al. (Eds.): ALIA 2016, CCIS 732, pp. 105–116, 2018.
https://doi.org/10.1007/978-3-319-90418-4_9

and prediction of risk [5,6]. The underlying problem is that many CDSSs cannot reliably represent the clinicians' mental model of how the system should work [7,8] i.e. accommodating clinicians' cognitive work flow [9]. Many intelligent agents lack a functional model allowing meaningful interpretation of results in terms of the features used for their risk classifications [10]. All these factors result in a reluctance to use such systems for major decision making tasks such as risk judgements because clinicians trust their own expertise and experience more than the complex models that underpin the intelligent systems [6,11].

To gain the trust of clinicians, CDSSs must support their cognitive work flow and mental models of decision-making [8,12]. This requires knowledge of how clinicians think and collect data, and how the data they collect work together to determine judgements of patients' health.

The ultimate goal of this research is to identify the most important cognitive reasoning factors upon which clinicians base their decisions. It does that by investigating how clinicians are alerted to the most pertinent information for evaluating risks. Their data-collection processes can then be simulated by intelligent agents so that they point assessors to the right data at the right time for making quick and effective clinical decisions.

The research analyses a database of patient profiles associated with clinical risk judgements in order to understand how the relationships within the data influence those judgements. It does not aim to introduce a new model or algorithm, but rather focuses on the theoretical investigations necessary for building a clinically justifiable model to be used for clinical intelligent agents. The paper will provide the study context and then explain the methodology in detail. The results will be described and discussed followed by conclusions and future work.

2   Context

The research was conducted on data collected by the Galatean Risk & Safety Tool, GRiST,[13] which is a clinical decision support system that helps assessors evaluate risks of suicide, self-harm, harm to others, self-neglect, and vulnerability. This study focused on suicide and used 30,000 cases of completed risk assessments provided by mental-health practitioners through their normal practice. The data are automatically stored without personal identification information before any researcher has access to them and so are completely anonymous from the start.[1]

GRiST is based on a psychological model of classification for representing clinical expertise [14]. The risk nodes such as suicide are hierarchical 'trees' that are deconstructed into progressively more granular concepts (branches) such as 'Current Intention' and 'Feelings & Emotions' until leaves of the tree are reached, such as anger and anxiety. Figure 1 shows a simplified part of the suicide risk tree.

---

[1] Ethics approval was obtained from NRES Committee East Midlands, 13/EM/0007, and Aston University.

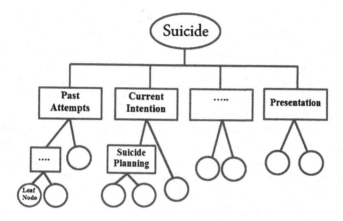

Fig. 1. Part of the suicide risk knowledge tree.

Although GRiST has several hundred leaf nodes, and therefore a very large potential data set for each patient, the actual number of questions is much lower because the tree provides a top-down gateway to the relevant concepts. For example, a top-level question is whether the patient has any history of suicide attempts and if the answer is 'NO' then all the history questions remain hidden and unasked. Hence the knowledge hierarchy imposes constraints on the order of asking questions because the branch questions have to be asked before the leaf questions are reached. When assessors have finished asking questions, they are asked to provide their overall risk judgement for the patient in the form of a score ranging from 0 (no risk) to 10 (maximum risk).

The idea is that not all the branches of the tree or all the questions of a branch are necessarily relevant for the patient under assessment. The task is to understand which branch variables (i.e. answers to branch questions) influence risk judgement, to what degree, and how these influences impact on the process of data collection. Data collection can then be guided only to those parts of the knowledge tree that are required for the particular risk assessment and particular patient under assessment, thereby minimising the number of questions needing to be asked. The specific objectives are to understand what drives the data collection behaviour of clinicians and use this to find a minimum set of variables required to provide accurate risk judgements for any particular patient.

3   Methodology

Bayes' Theorem describes how the degree of belief in an event should change to account for evidence and is widely utilised for analysing clinical decision making [15,16]. In this study, it was applied to understand how clinical judgements are affected by the sequence of data collection. The aim was to determine which questions would *change* the judgement the most, in the light of data already collected. Guiding assessors to these questions would provide the least number of questions required to provide the most informative risk evaluation.

The method is not as simple as described so far because each branch can have two answers, YES or NO, and they will not have the same influence on the posterior probability: the 'YES' answer may cause a large change with the 'NO' answer having no effect at all. Hence a question may only be useful for one answer but not the other and the likelihood of each answer affects the overall informativeness of the question. Furthermore, it was suspected that variables display different relationships when combined i.e. collected at the same time. Thus, the Bayesian conditional probability approach will be extended to investigate the variables' relationships on multiple levels and in different ways.

The conditional probability of an event 'A' given another event 'B' is denoted in this paper using the following format:

$$P(A|B) \text{ reads as probability of A given B.}$$

The condition (in the above example, B) is taken as the **I**ndependent **V**ariable, the IV, and the event whose probability we are trying to calculate (in the above example, A) is called the **D**ependent **V**ariable, the DV. Using this approach, the investigation was carried out in 2 main stages.

1. **Stage 1:** To investigate how answers to the questions of the knowledge tree influence clinicians' final risk judgement. First, we looked at how each variable changed the suicide risk judgement on its own, to give a measure of its predictive power. Second, we explored how variables change the probability of risk in combination with other variables, to find combinations of variables that are particularly predictive compared to each one separately.

2. **Stage 2:** To investigate the system (including the reasoning factors) with which clinicians evaluate the redundancy/informativeness of the variables. Using the findings of Stage 1, we define a number tests in order to decide which data are useful to collect and which data are redundant. The idea is that if clinicians stop asking questions in one part of the tree because of the answers they have obtained elsewhere, it should be possible to detect redundant parts of the tree. Assessors can then be guided away from these and towards more useful lines of questioning with respect to risk evaluation.

4   Findings

The risk judgements were categorised into three groups: High Risk (risk scores of 7 and above), Medium Risk (risk scores $4, 5, 6$) and Low Risk (risk scores of 3 and below). These groupings made it easier to measure the degree of dependency between variables and the risk by treating each risk group as a separate variable. Since determining the high risk patients is most important, the investigation concentrated on measuring the variables influence on High Risk. What follows is the result of analyses and the semantic conclusions drawn from them.

4.1   Stage 1: How Variables Influence Clinicians' Risk Judgement

With a total of 28 branch and sub-branch variables, 28 pairs of conditional probabilities of the risk given a question's answers were produced because only the "yes" answers were analysed (the "no" answers are, by definition, not indicative of high risk). Then the answers for each question were paired with answers for the other variables in combinations of pairs and triples. Any more than three variables reduces the sample size significantly and also became unmanageable in scale: 28 variables combined in groups of two produces 378 combinations and in groups of three produces 3,276 combinations based on combination factorial calculations. Each combination was then compared against the high risk variable to give a total number of 3,654 conditional probability calculations.

The combinations producing the most influence on high risk were selected, with a sample shown in Table 1. The table shows variables' influence on the probability of High Risk on an individual basis as well as jointly. The CP column gives the conditional probability of the DV given the IV and the change in the probability of DV caused by the IV is the fourth ΔP column. The change in probability, ΔP, shows how influential the variable is on the clinicians' risk judgements.

Table 1. A selection of most influential variables which individually or in combination influence clinicians' judgement of risk.

Independent variable	Dependant variable	CP	ΔP
Current Intention	High Risk	0.37	0.32
Presentation	High Risk	0.22	0.17
Suicide Triggers	High Risk	0.14	0.09
Ideation	High Risk	0.13	0.08
Self-Worth	High Risk	0.12	0.07
Motive & Engagement	High Risk	0.11	0.06
Feeling & Emotion	High Risk	0.09	0.04
Personality	High Risk	0.09	0.04
Presentation & Current Intention	High Risk	0.51	0.48
Current Intention & Suicide Planning	High Risk	0.46	0.41
Presentation & Self-Worth	High Risk	0.32	0.28
Presentation & Verbal Indicators	High Risk	0.30	0.25
Presentation & Personality	High Risk	0.22	0.17
Suicide ideation & Personality	High Risk	0.20	0.14

Figures 2 and 3 visualise the result of Table 1. Figure 2 shows the variables with strongest predictive power (influence) on the probability of High Risk on individual basis. Figure 3, on the other hand, shows the variable combinations with strongest predictive power on High Risk.

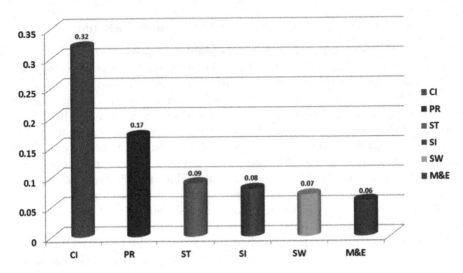

Fig. 2. Variables with strongest probability impact on High Risk on individual basis.

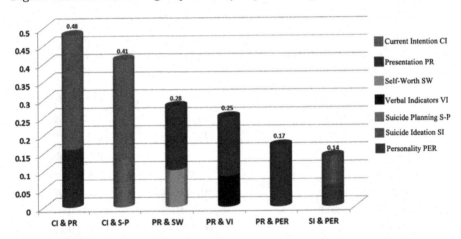

Fig. 3. Combination of variables with strongest probability impact on High Risk. Different proportion of colouring demonstrates the power of each variable in the combinations. For example the first column shows the combination of Current Intention and Presentation with Current Intention having a more impact on risk, hence the column is dominated in red. (Color figure online)

Table 1 and the associated figures reveal important insights into the clinicians' pattern of response. Some variables often appear in combinations with high predictive power as well as being strong independent predictors. It would make sense if these were primary drivers of clinical decisions and they include Current Intention to commit suicide (CI), Suicide Triggers (ST), Suicide Ideation (SI), Presentation of patients during assessment (PR), Self-Worth (SW) and Motivation & Engagement (M&E).

Furthermore, some variables' show increased predictive power in combination with other variables. For example, Self-Worth (SW), on its own, changes the probability of High Risk (HR) by 0.07 but when combined with the variable Presentation (PR) its influence on HR increases to 0.10:

$$\Delta P\Big(HR|SW\Big) = \mathbf{0.07} \quad \neq \quad \Delta P\Big((HR|PR)|SW\Big) = \mathbf{0.10}$$

$\implies$ SW demonstrates interactive behaviour with PR.

This means that when clinicians are concerned with the 'Presentation' of patients, asking about Self-Worth would increase clinicians' chance of judging the patients as high risk, if self worth was, indeed, an issue. To guide assessors to the most important data, the system needs to know both the independent influence of a variable and also how much it is likely to change the impact of risk in conjunction with others already asked. Interaction of variable influences is the key because the addition of a second or third IV sometimes influences the probability of high risk sometimes does not. For example, according to Table 1, Presentation, on its own changes the probability of High Risk by 0.17 but if the variable Personality (PER) is added, the risk is hardly affected (this is demonstrated in Fig. 3 by having the column representing Presentation and Personality as completely blue). However, when Personality is added to Suicide Ideation, the probability of High Risk increases by 0.07. It shows how the strength of interactions dynamically changes as new answers are added.

The results so far suggest that there are a limited number of features which strongly influence the clinical risk judgement. Furthermore, although the influences on risk change as new answers are added to previous ones, if the previous answers are already strong influencers, new answers make little difference: the strong influencers are making others redundant, which is an important factor in determining the order of data collection if minimising the questions required is important (which is the case for screening tools). This is investigated in more detail in Stage 2.

4.2 Stage 2: Identifying Redundant Variables

Having identified the most influential variables, it is important to clarify whether they mask all the other variables (hence make all other variables redundant) or whether there are certain combinations that will still be informative. It may also be the case that a particular variable is redundant for a certain sequence of answers but later becomes influential if a new one is added.

Redundancy was investigated using *Conditional Independence* between IVs and the DV: is the DV (high risk) independent of an IV when that IV occurs in conjunction with another IV? If so, then only the second IV is required. This can be written in terms of conditional probabilities as:

$$P(DV|IV2 \cap IV1) = P(DV|IV2)$$

where IV2 is the independent variable that is fully incorporating the influence of IV1. A variable can only be considered redundant if none of its answers (YES or

NO) can change the probability of the risk, given any answer (YES or NO) to the other variables. Therefore, the first redundancy test checks to see what effects the different answers for an IV would have on the redundancy of the other, test IV (T-IV).

Redundancy Test 1:

IF P (HR | IV=YES & T-IV) $\approx$ P (HR | IV=YES)

$\qquad$ AND $\qquad\qquad$ $\left.\right\}$ $\implies$ T-IV REDUNDANT

IF P (HR | IV=NO & T-IV) $\approx$ P (HR | IV=NO)

The second redundancy test examines the effects of different answers to the T-IV on redundancy of itself in relation to the risk. In other words, it checks to see how different answers to T-IV change its level of influence on the risk given that the first IV is present.

Redundancy Test 2:

IF P (HR | IV & T-IV = YES) $\approx$ P (HR | IV)

$\qquad$ AND $\qquad\qquad$ $\left.\right\}$ $\implies$ T-IV REDUNDANT

IF P (HR | IV & T-IV=NO) $\approx$ P (HR | IV)

The third test complements the previous two by checking to see if a variable which has been made (by the first two tests) redundant remains redundant permanently or whether it can become informative at a later point during the assessment when further variables have been collected.

Redundancy Test 3:

Given T-IV is redundant against IV

IF P(HR | IV & **additional IVs** & T-IV)

$\qquad\qquad$ $\approx$ $\qquad\qquad$ $\left.\right\}$ $\implies$ T-IV REDUNDANT

P (HR | IV1 & **additional IVs**)

The idea is that if the redundant features stay redundant throughout the assessment, then they can be removed from the sequence of questions. The method was tested using a selection of the strongest variables as found in Table 1 along with some of the weaker variables, with a variable deemed redundant if and only if it passes all the three redundancy tests.

The results were interesting: Some variables pass none of the tests, some pass the first test but not the second and some pass the first and second but not the third. For example, Tables 2, 3 and 4 show the result of the 3 redundancy tests on Current Intention, Presentation, Feeling & Emotion and Mental Faculty.

In these tests, Current Intention is taken as the IV and the other three are taken as the T-IVs. The tables show that Presentation is redundant if and only if Current Intention is given a NO value. Otherwise Presentation can independently change the level of risk. Presentation thus fails the first test of redundancy as demonstrated in Table 2 and is not investigated further. On the other hand, Feeling & Emotion passes the first test of redundancy, which gives the impression that as long as Current Intention is collected (whether its value is YES or NO) Feeling & Emotion is redundant. However it fails the second test (as demonstrated in Table 3) meaning Feeling & Emotion does not necessarily stay redundant if it has a NO value. In other words, while a YES value to Feeling & Emotion makes it redundant in the presence of either Current Intention answer, a NO value will actually make Feeling & Emotion informative (i.e. independently causes a substantial change on the probability of risk).

In contrast to Feeling & Emotion, Mental Faculty passes the first two tests. This means if Current Intention is collected (regardless of the value it takes), then Mental Faculty will always be redundant regardless of the value it is given (demonstrated by Tables 2 and 3). This might suggest that Mental Faculty is completely redundant but surprisingly Mental Faculty does not pass the third test. Table 4 shows that Mental Faculty which was previously made redundant with Current Intention, becomes informative ($\Delta P >$ Threshold) when a second

Table 2. First redundancy test applied to Presentation, Feeling & Emotion and Mental Faculty against Current Intention. Feeling & Emotion and Mental Faculty pass the test. Presentation fails the test as the change it causes on High Risk is **over** the threshold

Redundancy Test 1			
IV = Current Intention CI, T-IV = Presentation PR		ΔP	Threshold > 0.05
P(High Risk | CI = Yes & PR = YES) = 0.51 $\neq$	P(High Risk | CI = Yes) = 0.37	0.14	Over
P(High Risk | CI = NO & PR = YES) = 0.04 $\approx$	P(High Risk | CI = NO) = 0.01	0.03	Within
IV = Current Intention CI, T-IV = Feeling & Emotion FE		ΔP	Threshold > 0.05
P(High Risk | CI = Yes & FE = YES) = 0.39 $\approx$	P(High Risk | CI = Yes) = 0.37	0.02	Within
P(High Risk | CI = NO & FE = YES) = 0.02 $\approx$	P(High Risk | CI = NO) = 0.01	0.01	Within
IV = Current Intention CI, T-IV = Mental Faculty MF		ΔP	Threshold > 0.05
P(High Risk | CI = Yes & MF = YES) = 0.40 $\approx$	P(High Risk | CI = Yes) = 0.37	0.03	Within
P(High Risk | CI = NO & MF = YES) = 0.01 $\approx$	P(High Risk | CI = NO) = 0.01	0.0	Within

Table 3. Second redundancy test applied to Feeling & Emotion and Mental Faculty against Current Intention. Mental Faculty passes the test. Feeling & Emotion fails as the change it cases on High Risk is **over** the threshold when it is given a 'NO' answer

Redundancy Test 2			
IV = Current Intention CI, T-IV = Feeling & Emotion FE		ΔP	Threshold > 0.05
P(High Risk | CI = Yes & FE = YES) = 0.39 $\approx$	P(High Risk | CI = Yes) = 0.37	0.02	Within
P(High Risk | CI = YES & FE = NO) = 0.26 $\neq$	P(High Risk | CI = YES) = 0.37	0.11	Over
IV = Current Intention CI, T-IV = Mental Faculty MF		ΔP	Threshold > 0.05
P(High Risk | CI = Yes & MF = YES) = 0.40 $\approx$	P(High Risk | CI = Yes) = 0.37	0.03	Within
P(High Risk | CI = YES & MF = NO) = 0.37 $=$	P(High Risk | CI = YES) = 0.37	0.0	Within

Table 4. Third redundancy test applied to Mental Faculty against Current Intention. Mental Faculty fails the test as it regains its informativeness after being made redundant once.

Redundancy Test 3			
IV = Current Intention CI, T-IV = Mental Faculty MF Additional Variable = Feeling & Emotion FE		ΔP	Threshold > 0.05
P(High Risk | CI = Yes & MF = Yes) = 0.40	≈ P(High Risk | CI = Yes) = 0.37	0.03	Within
P(High Risk | CI = YES & FE = YES & MF = Yes) = 0.46	≠ P(High Risk | CI = YES& FE = Yes) = 0.39	0.07	Over

IV (i.e. Feeling & Emotion) is added to Current Intention. In other words, Mental Faculty comes back to be informative when Feeling & Emotion has been given a YES value. In clinical terms this means that when clinicians collect Current Intention and are also concerned with Feeling & Emotion, then the questions on Mental Faculty would influence their judgement of risk but not if they are not concerned with Feeling & Emotion.

These findings point out an important concept: the pattern of variable redundancy is not fixed but evolves throughout the assessment. In other words, a variable's redundancy (and informativeness) is a dynamic phenomenon and changes as the value to other variables become available.

4.3   Clinical Conclusions from the Result

This investigation provides preliminary suggestions about how clinical assessments might be optimised:

1. There is a group of features that always influence the clinical judgements and these are absolutely required in all contexts.
2. Depending on the context, which is dictated by the data collected during the course of the assessment, less influential features can actually be informative and hence required for evaluating the level of risk.
3. Clinicians do not evaluate the predictiveness of a variable in isolation from other variables. Rather, they base their evaluation on the combination of answers already obtained. Hence a new answer that is informative on its own can be completely redundant in the presence of other data because clinicians feel that the new information adds little or nothing to their existing understanding of the level of risk.
4. The informativeness of data fluctuates throughout an assessment. Not only does a variable's predictive power depend on the preceding variables but it can also change depending on the future data too. This dynamic life line is illustrated by Fig. 4.
5. The dynamic nature of data redundancy means the optimal order of asking questions is also dynamic: it has to be decided in real time.

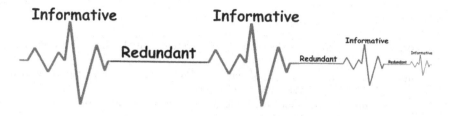

Fig. 4. Data informativeness life line

5   Conclusion and Future Work

In order for clinical decision support systems CDSSs to be effective, they have to be intelligent agents that simulate the clinical judgements of a human clinician. To achieve this, such intelligent agents have to be able to replicate clinicians' expertise and way of reasoning. This research has explored this aim by analysing a database of mental health risk assessments. The research aimed to understand the factors and circumstances influencing humans' (i.e. clinicians') decisions on the data they need to collect. Specifically, it tried to find out whether there is an optimal order of answers that produce the most accurate risk judgements with the least number of questions. This was pursued by analysing the probabilistic relationships between variables and clinical risk judgements at multiple levels.

The findings were used to extract key lessons about the way clinicians' risk judgements respond to the sequence of data collected. The most important is that the informativeness of variables have different patterns during the assessment. Some become redundant in the light of previous answers and will never then become informative; others are always informative; and some may be redundant with certain sequences of answers but then become informative in the light of a new answer, which means that their initial redundancy has not consigned them to the dustbin as far as asking the question. Hence, there is no fixed order of questions that will be the optimal one for all patients, which means the questions to be asked and the order in which they are to be asked have to be decided in real time.

The challenge is to use this extracted clinical intelligence to produce an intelligent decision support agent that is able to communicate with the human risk assessors, take input from them and then find and collect the best set of data features for each different patient and context. The model will then use the collected data and the induced knowledge to provide intelligent advice for the human assessors. Exactly how to do this is currently under investigation. One of the most significant outcomes will be a system that can provide screening questions and accompanying risk advice for people without a mental-health background, based on the inherent expertise of the clinical judgements residing in the GRiST database. It will be particularly useful for primary care and emergency services who have to make fast and reliable mental-health triage decisions for people in the community.

References

1. Pryor, T.A.: Development of decision support systems. Int. J. Clin. Monit. Comput. **7**(3), 137–146 (1990)
2. Campbell, H., Hotchkiss, R., Bradshaw, N., Porteous, M.: Integrated care pathways. BMJ Br. Med. J. **316**(7125), 133 (1998)
3. Fox, J., Patkar, V., Thomson, R.: Decision support for health care: the proforma evidence base. J. Innov. Health Inform. **14**(1), 49–54 (2006)
4. Kawamoto, K., Houlihan, C.A., Balas, E.A., Lobach, D.F.: Improving clinical practice using clinical decision support systems: a systematic review of trials to identify features critical to success. BMJ **330**(7494), 765 (2005)
5. Sanchez, F.: Suicide Explained: A Neuropsychological Approach. Xlibris Corporation (2007)
6. Brunton, K.: The evidence on how nurses approach risk assessment. Nurs. Times **101**(28), 38 (2005)
7. Kilsdonk, E., Peute, L.W., Riezebos, R.J., Kremer, L.C., Jaspers, M.W.M.: From an expert-driven paper guideline to a user-centred decision support system: a usability comparison study. Artif. Intell. Med. **59**(1), 5–13 (2013)
8. Peute, L.W.P., Jaspers, M.W.M.: The significance of a usability evaluation of an emerging laboratory order entry system. Int. J. Med. Inform. **76**(2), 157–168 (2007)
9. Sittig, D.F., Wright, A., Osheroff, J.A., Middleton, B., Teich, J.M., Ash, J.S., Campbell, E., Bates, D.W.: Grand challenges in clinical decision support. J. Biomed. Inform. **41**(2), 387–392 (2008)
10. Sampson, D.L., Parker, T.J., Upton, Z., Hurst, C.P.: A comparison of methods for classifying clinical samples based on proteomics data: a case study for statistical and machine learning approaches. PloS One **6**(9), e24973 (2011)
11. Dozois, D.J.A.: Psychological treatments: putting evidence into practice and practice into evidence. Can. Psychol./Psychologie canadienne **54**(1), 1 (2013)
12. Rezaei-Yazdi, A., Buckingham, C.D.: Understanding data collection behaviour of mental health practitioners. Stud. Health Technol. Inform. **207**, 193–202 (2014)
13. GRiST: Galatean risk and safety tool. www.egrist.org. Accessed 15 May 2014
14. Buckingham, C.D.: Psychological cue use and implications for a clinical decision support system. Med. Inform. Internet Med. **27**(4), 237–251 (2002)
15. Byers, S.N., Roberts, C.A.: Bayes' theorem in paleopathological diagnosis. Am. J. Phys. Anthropol. **121**(1), 1–9 (2003)
16. Spiegelhalter, D.J., Abrams, K.R., Myles, J.P.: Bayesian Approaches to Clinical Trials and Health-Care Evaluation, vol. 13. Wiley, Chichester (2004)

Identifying Human-Like Qualities
for Non-player Characters

Jason A. Hall[1(✉)], Llyr Ap Cenydd[2], and Christopher J. Headleand[1]

[1] University of Lincoln, Lincolnshire, England, UK
{jahall,cheadleand}@lincoln.ac.uk
[2] Bangor University, Gwynedd, Wales, UK
http://staff.lincoln.ac.uk/cheadleand

Abstract. This research investigates qualities common to non-player characters in games can contribute towards an in-game agents believability. A number of NPCs with different initial setups were evaluated using a blind Turing Test style evaluation, in which players were pitted against another human and different AI controlled NPCs over six rounds. At the end of each round, players were asked to rate both opponents, unknowing which was human or NPC. The results demonstrated that none of the agents were able to reliably fool the player, however, some combinations of characteristics were successful in generating behaviour that was perceived as 'human-like'.

Keywords: Non-playable characters · Artificial Intelligence
Believability · Presence

1 Introduction

Non-player characters (NPCs) are autonomous game agents that act independently of the player [1]. NPCs and are often used to enhance the game experience, and the perceived believability of human-like non-player characters (NPCs) is often of great concern to modern video game designers [2]. Furthermore the recent resurgence of virtual reality is allowing developers to invoke ever increasing levels of immersion [3], where believable NPCs could greatly affect suspension of disbelief [4] and help maintain a sense of presence in the virtual world [5].

As the behaviour of NPCs is often parameterised, could these parameters be modified to produce behaviour that is considered more believable by the player? As there are many aspects to how an NPC's behaviour is structured, insight is needed to understand how parameters influence the synthesis of believable behaviour. Furthermore, with greater understanding in this area, an NPC's behaviour could be generated procedurally, potentially facilitating a diverse spectrum of believable behaviours.

The purpose of this research is to evaluate a number of characteristics that NPCs can have and how they produce a sense of believability. We start by providing an overview of the related work, before describing our experiment

© Springer International Publishing AG, part of Springer Nature 2018
P. R. Lewis et al. (Eds.): ALIA 2016, CCIS 732, pp. 117–129, 2018.
https://doi.org/10.1007/978-3-319-90418-4_10

method including the design of the NPC agents. We then present the results of the experiment and offer our conclusions.

2   Background

2.1   What is Believability?

Demeure et al. [6] state that *"believability* is often used to describe expectations concerning virtual agents". Ortega et al. [7] stated that the higher the level of believability within a virtual agent, the more immersed and satisfied a player would be within a populated virtual environment. Xuetao et al. [8] also found that more believable agents produce an increased satisfaction in users.

Thomas and Johnston, two principal animators of Disney, stated that the main goal of believable characters is to provide the *illusion of life* [9]. The real world is full of life, and agents should attempt to replicate this quality and make a virtual world feel alive and immersive. The 'believability' of a character may not require realism in their visual representation [10]; a sentiment echoed by Doyle and Mateas [11,12] who argue that a character need only be realistic in the context of it's environment.

Achieving believability in video games can be more complex, because of the increased level of player agency. Players can be embodied in the game through avatars allowing them to directly interact with virtual characters [5]. Therefore, when designing human-like agents, one objective is for the synthetic human to act like a real human [13,14]. If a player is able to believe that the environment, and the entities that they interact with are real then the virtual environment's level of immersion is said to trigger a sense of 'Presence' [15].

The believability of agents can directly affect whether a user can achieve a temporary suspension of disbelief [16]. In this context, the suspension of disbelief is when a person does not question the agent's existence as a real entity voluntarily. Games often describe believability in one of three ways, often categorised as character, role and player believability. Character believability is the belief that the character is a living being [17]. Role believability is the belief that the behaviour exhibited by the character is appropriate for the role they are portraying. Finally, player believability is the belief that a human is controlling the character [4].

2.2   Autonomy

Thalmann et al. [18] and Guy et al. [19] state that autonomy is essential for designing believable human-like agents. Autonomy increases the believability of agents, as making them autonomous significantly reduces their predictability [20]. Predictable behaviour is often described as 'robotic', which is a distinctly non-human-like quality.

Vision and Hearing. The hearing and visual capability of humans varies considerably, dependant on several contributory factors, with age being one of the biggest contributors. With this in mind, when developing an agent to be human-like, their sensory ability should be limited to that of the intended player. Typically an agent imitating the capabilities of an elderly human would have lower levels of vision and hearing than that of an agent imitating the capabilities of younger person.

When developing agents with realistic hearing and vision, it must be ensured that they do not have senses which allow them to sense aspects of their environment that humans are incapable of sensing. This means that agents should not have superhuman omnipresence, or additional sensory capability, as the agent's behaviour would be inhuman and therefore have reduced believability [13].

2.3   Parameters

In the literature, a number of studies mention interpersonal distance and reaction time as being key parameters for the believability of an agent. For this reason, the following background is included in greater detail.

Interpersonal Distance. Interpersonal distance (IPD), is the distance that people choose to keep between themselves and other people. The distance is smaller for friends and family than it is for strangers [21].

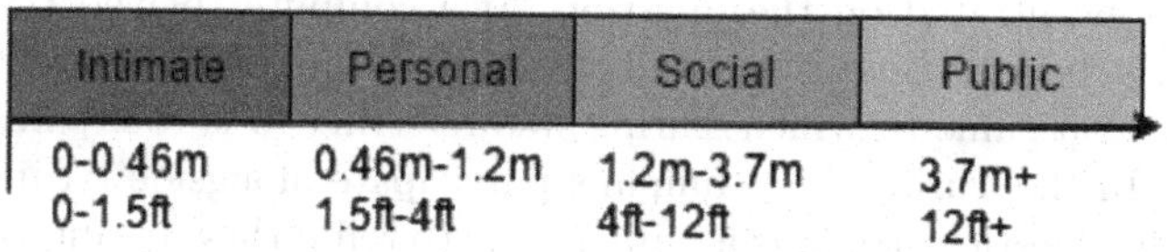

Intimate	Personal	Social	Public
0-0.46m	0.46m-1.2m	1.2m-3.7m	3.7m+
0-1.5ft	1.5ft-4ft	4ft-12ft	12ft+

Fig. 1. The four zones which make up interpersonal distance [22].

As shown in Fig. 1, the left-most zone is the proximity only the closest individuals would be comfortable, with the level of comfort increasing rightwards with distance depending on social situation. [22]. It has been stated that multiple factors such as culture [22], race, gender [23], age [24] and affiliation [25] can also affect the ranges of each zone. Yee et al. [26] stated that established findings of IPD are represented similarly in virtual environments, with the example that male-male dyads have larger IPDs than female-female dyads. In this scenario, IPD decreases are compensated with gaze avoidance as predicted by the Equilibrium Theory, in order to reduce undesired intimacy and return to an equilibrium state.

However, in a game world these rules may be different. In certain circumstances (such as a game involving hand to hand combat) it may be considered normal for players to move very close to each other. On the other hand, in other game types (for example, those involving long range combat) greater distance than usual norms may be required to achieve believability.

Reaction Time. Vinayagamoorthy et al. [27] state that if an agent is unable to react to certain situations in an appropriate amount of time, the level of believability of that agent significantly decreases. This is because humans are capable of responding to actions given a reasonable amount of time to process how to react.

'Artificial Stupidity' is implemented in game agents in order to ensure that they are only capable of doing what humans can do, and are usually much worse to balance between fun and challenge. Le Hy et al. [13] stated that an important criterion is that the synthetic character does not cheat and that its perceptions and actions should be as human player-like as possible. In virtual environments without artificial stupidity, an agent could process a player's actions much quicker than a typical human, and react far too quickly for the behaviour to appear human-like, thereby reducing believability significantly [13,28].

Agents must also be able to react appropriately, at times when any contact occurs with the player or other agents, and ensure that the reaction is not overly exaggerated, such as overly stiff or loose reactions that could also break immersion [29].

2.4   Assessment

The Turing Test was first proposed by Alan Turing in 1950 [30]. Turing's intention was to sidestep the philosophical question "Can a Machine Think?" as it would involve knowing precise definitions of the words 'machine' and 'think' [31]. Instead, he concentrated on the question "If a computer played the imitation game, would it be indistinguishable from a human player's perspective?".

The imitation game to which Turing was referring to is today known as the Turing Test. In the Turing Test, humans participate alongside AI in a series of questions. The question being, is a human able to tell if they are interacting with another human or an artificial agent, when within a virtual environment? This question later took the form of the Loebner Prize [32]. The method of assessing the believability of the agents participating was whether they could convince a panel of judges that they were conversing with a human, rather than an AI-controlled agent. The agreed pass mark for this method is generally set at 30%, meaning 3 out of 10 judges would have to be convinced.

The 'Bot Prize' competition is similar to the Turing test for intelligent agents, in the respect that human judges are tasked to identify whether their opponents in the game were human players or virtual agents [33]. The 2K Bot Prize competition was held at the IEEE Symposium on Computational Intelligence and Games in 2008. The platform of this competition was the first person shooter Unreal Tournament 2004 (UT2004). The task was for agents to be the most 'believable' of all of the contesting bots, showing the most human-like behaviour, whilst still being able to adapt to gameplay. Five teams entered the final competition [33].

From 2008 until 2010 the Bot Prize followed the standard Turing Test format of one human judge, one computer program, and one human confederate per match. Judges designated one opponent from each match as a human and rated each opponent on a humanness scale [34].

Hingston [35] describes a variation of the Turing Test which was implemented in the 2010 Bot Prize. In this test, the judges were equipped with a 'devastating weapon'. This weapon could be shot by the judge at a particular player if they believed that the player was not human. If a human player was shot then the shooter would instantly be killed in-game and lose 10 points. This was to ensure that the weapon could not be used to eventually identify bots. The test assessed whether the agents were believable by considering if they were able to hide amongst the human players.

To perform well in the competition, an agent needed to act as human-like as possible, including having human-like capabilities such as being able to adapt to some changes made throughout the game, whilst also being fallible. The goal of the competition was to see if computer game bots can fool human judges into believing they are human at least 50% of the time [34].

3   Method and Design

Eight participants (6 Male and 2 Female) between the ages of 18 and 38, from European backgrounds were recruited for our experiment. The experiment results are only applicable to this demographic and therefore cannot guarantee similar results with different participant groups. All participants performed the same number of rounds, and had the same human opposition as all other participants for all six rounds.

Two computers were setup with instances of the game installed, one controlled by the human participant, and the other by the human opponent. The game environment was a flat world, with procedurally generated obstacles, each round lasted between 2–3 min.

Before beginning the experiment, the aim of the experiment, and the controls and the mechanics within the game were explained to the participants. They were also informed that another human would be playing alongside them, but were not informed of which in-game character the human opponent was controlling.

3.1   Game Overview

The test-bed game was a 'death-match' style first person shooter. This was selected because it placed the player in an environment where they are forced to interact with multiple opponents. A number of related studies have utilised this game type for this reason [31]. The implementation and source code used in this study is unavailable to the public at this time.

(a) An instance of the game map.   (b) The player perspective of the two opponents.

Each game started with the participant entering the game alongside another human player and an AI-controlled agent. Each individual character in each instance of the game were given a unique colour, randomly assigned for each game. Each participant played six rounds, each round having a different AI-controlled agent (the specifics of which are detailed in the following section). The participant and the other human player were located in different spaces so that they could not see the other player's screen or reactions.

At the end of each round, the subject was asked to score the following aspects of both in-game characters that they were pitted against on a scale of 1–5 (5 being the highest and 1 being the lowest): Aggressiveness, Intelligence, Difficulty and Human-likeness.

3.2 Parameterised AI

The behaviour of the AI opponents was based on a number of key parameters. These were *Interpersonal Distance (IPD), Reaction Time, Complexity of Tactics (COT) and Hostility*. The four parameters were selected as they were identified in the literature as factors that contribute towards believability.

IPD defined how close the character is able to get to the opponent. Low IPD allows the agent to become close to their opponent, while high IPD makes them more wary of their opponent and keep a greater distance.

Hostility determined the behaviour while the agent was shooting at the target. Those with high hostility would have an increased chance to reduce the distance between the opponent, with the aim of reducing the chance of missing their opponent, whereas those with a low hostility would have an increased chance of staying stationary to shoot from distance.

COT determined how the agents would choose their targets when multiple opponents were in their vision at the same time. An agent with low COT had an increased chance of going for the target directly in front, whereas those with high COT would have an increased chance to target the closest opponent.

Reaction Time determined when an agent sees the opponent and how long it would take for them to decide whether to rush towards the opponent or stand their ground. The larger the reaction time value, the longer it would take for the agent to react.

IPD represented the distance away from other agents that the character maintained as a minimum. However, the other three characteristics were probability-based. The higher the value, the less likely a specific behaviour was to be activated.

Vinayagamoorth et al. [27] state that if an agent is unable to react to certain situations in an appropriate amount of time, or merely lack a variety of responses, the level of believability of that agent significantly decreases due to the fact that humans are unique and have limitless variety in their responses. Yee et al. [26] theorised that simulating interpersonal distance may lead to an increase in believability. Tencé et al. [5] stated that a video game's complexity of interactions impacts on the believability of agents. If interactions between the players, agents and the game are few, it may be hard to assess believability. Therefore, choice of target and deciding on the execution of attacking the target are very important.

Play-testing was used to establish values for each of these parameters to create six distinct (playable) characters that are detailed in the following subsection.

3.3   Characters

A common interface script was used for both the AI and human controllers. This determined standard navigation and vision to ensure that both the humans and the AI's had the same basic abilities. All characters used the same model and key-framed animations. A shooting code segment was also implemented with built-in range and accuracy limitations. The vision for the AI-controlled agents involved casting a fan of rays forward, and $60°$ either side from the NPC (emulating the players perspective from a monitor). If any of the NPC's ray-casts intersected another object or agent, the AI character became aware of it.

The six different character parameter setups were as follows:

P.E.A:
Hostility: 80
IPD: 2.5
CoT: 25
Reaction Time: 150

E.I:
Hostility: 50
IPD: 10
CoT: 25
Reaction Time: 75

H.I.V.E:
Hostility: 80
IPD: 10
CoT: 80
Reaction Time: 150

S.D.A:
Hostility: 25
IPD: 7
CoT: 80
Reaction Time: 40

Q.T:
Hostility: 25
IPD: 7
CoT: 80
Reaction Time: 150

L.O.V.E:
Hostility: 25
IPD: 2.5
CoT: 25
Reaction Time: 40

4   Results

The results indicate that the agents were unable to mimic human-like behaviour to the degree that they could be reliably mistaken as a human player. This is demonstrated by all of the agents falling short of human likeness when compared to the real human player (See Fig. 5).

The mode rating for the human character was 4, across each of four areas rated by the participants. While some of the agents were able to equal this in specific areas, none were capable of matching it for all parameters. However, throughout the experiment, there were *eight* instances where the participants rated the overall human-likeness of AI higher than the human. On three occasions the characteristic set E.I was rated more human-like than the human player.

The Cronbach's alpha demonstrates internal consistency in the results with a value of 0.9167. A Spearmans Rank test showed no correlation between any of the AI parameters values and the assessment scores.

4.1   Aggressiveness

The results of our experiment imply that the player's perception of aggressiveness was more complex than the basic definition upon which the hostility implementation was based. While there appears to be some link there is no strong correlation.

The players perception of the agent's aggressiveness appears to be a combination of multiple characteristics. These results suggest that the reason for H.I.V.E and P.E.A having the highest aggressiveness was due to the current implementation's use of high levels of hostility and reaction time characteristics.

Furthermore, the results show that the least aggressive agent was S.D.A (see Fig. 2), an agent with low hostility and reaction time. Interestingly, the agent named L.O.V.E; who had equally the lowest hostility and reaction time in it's characteristic set, was perceived to be more aggressive than the agent named E.I, a characteristic set who held much larger values of both hostility and reaction time.

The agent named Q.T had a similar anomaly, with it only having a hostility value of 25, the agent was perceived to be equally as aggressive as E.I on average and obtained a higher median aggressiveness rating. This encourages the thought that the reaction time characteristic affects the perceived aggressiveness more than the current implementation of hostility, as Q.T's reaction time is double E.I's reaction time and the hostility of Q.T is half of E.I's hostility. This conclusion is further encouraged by the fact that both E.I and Q.T agents held higher reaction time values than the lowest rated hostility characteristic set (S.D.A).

L.O.V.E and Q.T were able to match the human opponent's mode in aggressiveness (4). All but one of the remaining agents had a mode of three. However, S.D.A was bimodal, holding the values two and four and so was simultaneously the highest and lowest rated.

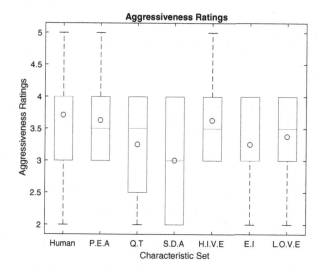

Fig. 2. Average aggressiveness rating for the human and AI opponents, note that the circle denotes the mean score.

4.2   Difficulty

In Fig. 3, the results show that L.O.V.E was overall the most difficult agent to compete against (average rating of 3.625), including the other human player (average rating of 3.5). This is an interesting result because L.O.V.E was deemed the least intelligent (See Fig. 4) of the agents (including the human). This implies that players did not necessarily consider difficulty to be a major contributing factor towards the intelligence of the agent. However, it is worth noting that there was only a .625 difference between the mean scores the agent identified as most difficult (L.O.V.E) and the one considered least difficult (Q.T).

4.3   Intelligence

In Fig. 4, the results show that S.D.A appeared the most intelligent agent through obtaining an mean perceived intelligence rating of 3.5 (only 0.083 less than the mean intelligence rating of the human). L.O.V.E appeared to be the least intelligent out of the AI agents (2.75 mean intelligence rating). However, the modes of all results suggest that the participants thought that most of the agents were able to exhibit in-game intelligence on a par with the human opponent.

The results imply that the average player's perception of intelligence is similar to what is produced by a combination of high interpersonal distance and high complexity of tactics (by our definitions).

4.4   Human Likeness

There is little difference between the top three NPC's (S.D.A, P.E.A, and E.I) in terms of human likeness, and none of which had a mean higher than the

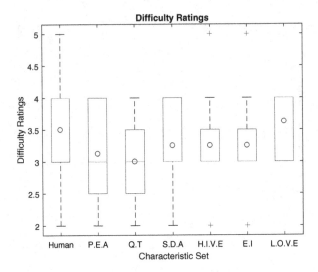

Fig. 3. Average difficulty rating for the human and AI opponents

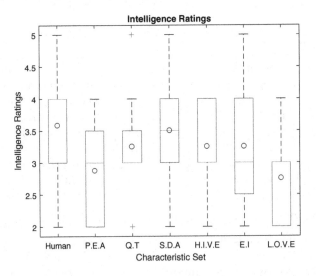

Fig. 4. Average intelligence rating for the human and AI opponents

human participant - as shown in Fig. 5. However, E.I and the human participant both had modes of 4. All agents were also rated more human-like than the true human opponent on at least one occasion. S.D.A had the highest mean for human-likeness out of the AI agents. The results are rather peculiar given that S.D.A has significantly different in parameters to the second and third most human-like and notably, it was rated the least aggressive of all the agents, while the human opponent was rated the most agressive.

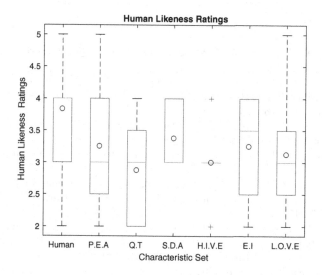

Fig. 5. Average overall human-likeness rating for the human and AI opponents

5   Conclusions

In this paper, six characteristic sets of agents were constructed in order to attempt to identify which characteristics contributed to the believability in human-likeness in video-game agents. Eight individuals played against all six of the AI-controlled agents; one for each of the six rounds, and assessed their aggressiveness, difficulty, intelligence and overall human-likeness on a scale of 1–5.

Overall, this experiment's results imply that combinations of characteristics present the player with differing behaviours such as:

1. High hostility and complexity of tactics create more difficult characters.
2. High interpersonal distance and high complexity of tactics creates characters that are perceived to be more intelligent.

With regards to believability in the form of human-likeness, this could not be narrowed to a single parameter but instead emerges out of a number of parameters. This implies that within a death-match environment, agents with certain combinations of characteristics are able to exhibit stronger qualities for specific metrics. It should be noted that the results are limited in scope, and only applicable to the game mode used in the experiment, and thus may vary with differing game modes and types. However, we argue that the results justify further research in this area.

In this study, we pre-defined a number of characteristics. However, the results show that there was no single characteristic that explains any of the results in the metrics we were evaluating. Future work would explore a much wider range of settings in a larger study, and potentially use machine learning techniques to develop the ideal agent based on our parameter set.

References

1. Connolly, T.M.: Psychology, Pedagogy, and Assessment in Serious Games. IGI Global, Hershey (2013)
2. Lankoski, P., Björk, S.: Gameplay design patterns for believable non-player characters. In: Situated Play: Proceedings of the 2007 Digital Games Research Association Conference, pp. 416–423 (2007)
3. Bowman, D.A., McMahan, R.P.: Virtual reality: how much immersion is enough? Computer 40(7), 36–43 (2007)
4. Livingstone, D.: Turing's test and believable AI in games. Computers in Entertainment (CIE) 4(1), 6 (2006)
5. Tencé, F., Buche, C., De Loor, P., Marc, O.: The challenge of believability in video games: Definitions, agents models and imitation learning. arXiv preprint arXiv:1009.0451 (2010)
6. Demeure, V., Niewiadomski, R., Pelachaud, C.: How is believability of a virtual agent related to warmth, competence, personification, and embodiment? Presence Teleoperators Virtual Environ. 20(5), 431–448 (2011)
7. Ortega, J., Shaker, N., Togelius, J., Yannakakis, G.N.: Imitating human playing styles in super mario bros. Entertainment Comput. 4(2), 93–104 (2013)
8. Xuetao, M., Bouchet, F., Sansonnet, J.P.: Impact of agent's answers variability on its believability and human-likeness and consequent chatbot improvements. In: Proceedings of AISB, pp. 31–36 (2009)
9. Thomas, F., Johnston, O.: Disney Animation: The Illusion of Life. Abbeville, New York (1981)
10. Imbert, R., Sánchez, M.I., de Antonio, A., Segovia, J.: The amusement internal modelling for believable behaviour of avatars in an intelligent virtual environment. In: ECAI 1998, Workshop in Intelligent Virtual Environments, Citeseer (1998)
11. Doyle, P.: Believability through context using knowledge in the world to create intelligent characters. In: Proceedings of the First International Joint Conference on Autonomous Agents and Multiagent Systems: part 1, pp. 342–349. ACM (2002)
12. Mateas, M.: An Oz-Centric review of interactive drama and believable agents. In: Wooldridge, M.J., Veloso, M. (eds.) Artificial Intelligence Today. LNCS (LNAI), vol. 1600, pp. 297–328. Springer, Heidelberg (1999). https://doi.org/10.1007/3-540-48317-9_12
13. Le Hy, R., Arrigoni, A., Bessière, P., Lebeltel, O.: Teaching Bayesian behaviours to video game characters. Robot. Auton. Syst. 47(2), 177–185 (2004)
14. Togelius, J., Yannakakis, G.N., Karakovskiy, S., Shaker, N.: Assessing believability. In: Hingston, P. (ed.) Believable Bots, pp. 215–230. Springer, Heidelberg (2013)
15. Magnenat-Thalmann, N., Kim, H., Egges, A., Garchery, S.: Believability and interaction in virtual worlds. In: Multi-Media Modeling Conference, International, pp. 2–9. IEEE Computer Society (2005)
16. Bates, J.: The nature of characters in interactive worlds and the Oz project. Carnegie Mellon University Pittsburgh, PA, School of Computer Science (1992)
17. Bates, J., et al.: The role of emotion in believable agents. Commun. ACM 37(7), 122–125 (1994)
18. Thalmann, D.: Challenges for the research in virtual humans. In: Proceedings of AGENTS 2000. Number VRLAB-CONF-2007-064 (2000)
19. Guye-Vuilleme, A., Thalmann, D.: A high-level architecture for believable social agents. Virtual Reality 5(2), 95–106 (2000)

20. Luck, M., Aylett, R.: Applying artificial intelligence to virtual reality: intelligent virtual environments. Appl. Artif. Intell. **14**(1), 3–32 (2000)
21. Holland, R.W., Roeder, U.R., Brandt, A.C., Hannover, B., et al.: Don't stand so close to me the effects of self-construal on interpersonal closeness. Psychol. Sci. **15**(4), 237–242 (2004)
22. Hall, E.T.: The Hidden Dimension. Doubleday, New York (1966)
23. Rosegrant, T.J., McCroskey, J.C.: The effects of race and sex on proxemic behavior in an interview setting. South. J. Commun. **40**(4), 408–418 (1975)
24. Willis Jr., F.N.: Initial speaking distance as a function of the speakers' relationship. Psychon. Sci. **5**(6), 221–222 (1966)
25. Evans, G.W., Howard, R.B.: Psychol. Bull. Personal space **80**(4), 334 (1973)
26. Yee, N., Bailenson, J.N., Urbanek, M., Chang, F., Merget, D.: The unbearable likeness of being digital: the persistence of nonverbal social norms in online virtual environments. Cyber Psychol. Behav. **10**(1), 115–121 (2007)
27. Vinayagamoorthy, V., Gillies, M., Steed, A., Tanguy, E., Pan, X., Loscos, C., Slater, M., et al.: Building Expression into Virtual Characters (2006)
28. Silverman, B.G., McDonald, D., Lazarus, R., Leung, A., Hussain, T., Bharathy, G., Eidelson, R.J., Pelechano Gómez, N., Sandhaus, E., et al.: Interoperable Human Behavior Models for Simulations (2006)
29. Allen, B., Chu, D., Shapiro, A., Faloutsos, P.: On the beat!: timing and tension for dynamic characters. In: Proceedings of the 2007 ACM SIGGRAPH/Eurographics symposium on Computer animation, Eurographics Association, pp. 239–247 (2007)
30. Turing, A.M.: Computing machinery and intelligence. In: Mind, pp. 433–460 (1950)
31. Hingston, P.: A turing test for computer game bots. IEEE Trans. Comput. Intell. AI Games **1**(3), 169–186 (2009)
32. Mauldin, M.L.: Chatterbots, tinymuds, and the turing test: Entering the loebner prize competition. In: AAAI, vol. 94, pp. 16–21 (1994)
33. Wang, D., Subagdja, B., Tan, A.H., Ng, G.W.: Creating human-like autonomous players in real-time first person shooter computer games. In: Proceedings of Twenty-First Annual Conference on Innovative Applications of Artificial Intelligence, pp. 173–178 (2009)
34. Schrum, J., Karpov, I.V., Miikkulainen, R.: Ut$\hat{2}$: human-like behavior via neuroevolution of combat behavior and replay of human traces. In: IEEE Conference on Computational Intelligence and Games (CIG) 2011, pp. 329–336. IEEE (2011)
35. Hingston, P.: A new design for a turing test for bots. In: IEEE Symposium on Computational Intelligence and Games (CIG) 2010, pp. 345–350. IEEE (2010)

Applications and Games

Governing Narrative Events with Tropes as Institutional Norms

Matt Thompson[1]([✉]), Julian Padget[1], and Steve Battle[2]

[1] Department of Computer Science, University of Bath, Bath, UK
{m.r.thompson,j.a.padget}@bath.ac.uk
[2] Department of Computer Science and Creative Technologies,
University of the West of England, Bristol, UK
steve.battle@uwe.ac.uk

Abstract. A narrative world can be viewed as a form of society in which characters follow a set of social norms whose collective function is to guide the characters through (the creation of) a story arc and reach some conclusion. By modelling the rules of a narrative using norms, we can govern the actions of agents that act out the characters in a story. Agents are given sets of permitted actions and obligations to fulfil based on their and the story's current situation. However, a way to describe stories in terms of social norms is needed. Existing formalisms for narrative do not work at multiple layers of abstraction, and do not provide a rich enough vocabulary for describing stories. We use story tropes as a means of building reusable story components with which we describe the social norms that govern our storyworld agents.

1 Introduction

A satisfying narrative must be more than just a series of interactions between character agents. There is a need for some underlying structure to these interactions. Additionally, agents are not a natural way to model events such as off-screen occurrences or scene introductions from a narrator.

Simulating a narrative using intelligent agents as characters offers many advantages. Each agent can be programmed to behave in certain idiosyncratic ways, based on a psychological or behavioural model. A common approach to add narrative structure to an agent-based simulation is to implement a drama manager, as in Mateas and Sterns' *Façade* [7].

This presents a problem: if the agents are being governed by a drama manager, to what extent are they autonomous? Do they still have some degree of 'free will' to carry out their own individual actions, in accordance with their personalities?

Other approaches to balancing authorial control with player or character agency include the use of director agents [5], reincorporation of player actions back into the narrative [12] and mediation to prevent narrative-breaking actions [9].

In this report we present an approach to regulating narrative structure while still allowing agents some degree of autonomy. The narrative world is described and managed using an institutional model. An author creates the institutional model by constructing it out of story tropes.

© Springer International Publishing AG, part of Springer Nature 2018
P. R. Lewis et al. (Eds.): ALIA 2016, CCIS 732, pp. 133–137, 2018.
https://doi.org/10.1007/978-3-319-90418-4_11

An institutional model can be thought of as a model of society. By specifying a set of social norms, certain agent behaviours can be encouraged or discouraged according to the needs of that society. Institutions have been used to simulate the workings of auctions [2], vehicle convoys [1] and crowd movement [4]. All these applications are similar in that they all involve intelligent agents working together in a social environment.

The advantages of using institutions to govern agents' behaviours is that they still allow the agents some autonomy in their actions. The rules of a society are implied, and while adherence to these rules is encouraged, it is possible for them to be broken (often incurring a penalty). This makes them ideal for regimenting the actions of characters in a narrative. In order to have a narrative that is satisfying and consistent with a certain story world, some kind of structure is needed. However, if this narrative is to be interactive, the characters within the narrative need some degree of freedom in their actions. They need the ability to bend or break the rules of the storyworld at times, in order to surprise the player. Institutions make this possible for the agents to do. However, as with breaking the rules of any society, diverging from the norm may bring penalties and hardship upon the deviating agent.

The advantages of using tropes are that they provide a way of constructing story models at several levels of abstraction. Small, composable components can be described by authors (using either a domain-specific language or user interface) and re-used. Additionally, most authors are familiar with the concept of tropes (as described in Sect. 4).

2   Using Tropes as Story Components

Many narrative formalisms exist in the field of interactive narrative research. Propp's seminal work "The Morphology of the Folktale" [8], though first published in 1928, is still a widely-used formalism for researchers and game designers looking to generate narratives procedurally. Propp identifies recurring characters and motifs in Russian folklore, distilling them down to a concise syntax with which to describe stories.

Propp defines a total of 31 distinct story functions, some of which can have subtle variations from story to story. Each function is given a number and symbol in order to create a succinct way of describing entire stories.

These functions are enacted by characters following certain roles. Each role (or *dramatis personae* in Propp's definition) has a *sphere of action* consisting of the functions that they are able to perform at any point in the story. Propp defines seven roles that have distinct spheres of action: *villain, donor, helper, princess, dispatcher, hero,* and *false hero.*

However, Propp's formalism is limited in its expressiveness. Creating new story functions goes against his system, and even if such a technique were possible, an author would not be able to compose new story functions from a combination of other story functions. This means that Propp does not provide us with any means of abstraction for creating story descriptions.

Other, more modern approaches suffer the same problem. Lehnert's plot units are another commonly-used narrative formalism [6]. However, these plot units only describe stories as three types of event: positive, negative and mental. These events occur with respect to a single character in the story, so an author must always author story components with concrete characters in mind. Furthermore, the order of composition must always be in a certain sequence, and plot units cannot refer to other plot units. Again, we are left without a means of creating abstractions for our story components.

We use story tropes as a method of creating story components. Tropes are recurring motifs, themes and clichés that appear in stories. Examples are *The Hero's Journey*, where an adventurer receives a call to adventure, taking them away from home and into the land of adventure and *The Evil Empire*, where a large organisation tries its best to stop the hero at any cost.

Hundreds of natural-language descriptions of Tropes appear on the TVTropes website [13], which we translate into formal (deontic) logical statements. The key advantage of using tropes is the fact that tropes can contain other tropes, enabling us to create abstractable, expressive story components. These logical statements are then used to create social institutions with which to govern the character agents.

3 Institutions for Narrative Regulation

Early examples of institutional models suggest their application to the regulation of systems involving multiple actors. Noriega's "fish market" thesis describes the application of an agent-mediated institution for regulating a fish market auction scenario [2], checking the validity of agent actions and addressing the issue of agent accountability in an auction environment. Rodriguez-Aguilar [10], and later Vázquez-Salceda [14], refine and extend Noriega's implementation of agent-mediated institutions.

However, it is Cliffe's approach of using Answer Set Programming (ASP) to specify institutions that we use here [3]. We define an institution in terms of *deontic logic*, specifying the permissions and obligations that act upon agents at any particular point in the story.

This approach alone is not enough, however. In order to effectively model a narrative using an institution and ASP, we must use a formalism for narrative that specifies which events and actions occur at certain points in the narrative. We achieve this by translating trope descriptions from the TVTropes [13] website into actions that agents are permitted or obliged to perform.

Tropes are described in TropICAL (the TROPe Interactive Chronical Language), which compiles to InstAL [3], an action language for deontic logic that generates ASP code. An example TropICAL trope description is shown in Listing 1.1. The generated code is run through a solver after each story event to determine the permissions and obligations that hold on each character at the next point in the story. We also provide StoryBuilder, a user interface that authors can use to create tropes and arrange them to create interactive stories.

Listing 1.1: The Hero's Journey described in TropICAL

```
1   "The-Hero's-Journey" is a Trope where:
2     The Hero is at Home
3     Then the Hero meets the Dispatcher
4     Then the Hero must go to the Land Of Adventure before the
          Villain kills the Victim
5       Otherwise, the Story must end
6     When the Hero is at the Land Of Adventure:
7       The Hero may kill the Villain
8         Or the Villain may escape
9     Then the Hero returns Home
```

4   Evaluation

The work was presented to the Oxford and London Interactive Fiction meetup group organised by Emily Short [11]. Participants in the group consisted of mainly game developers and interactive story authors, using tools such as Unity, Twinery and Inform to construct their interactive stories. The presentation consisted of a description of the trope DSL (TropICAL) and institution-governed multi-agent system, as well as a demonstration of the StoryBuilder UI. Afterwards, a questionnaire was handed to participants.

The questionnaire, though being a preliminary qualitative evaluation of the work, showed promise in our approach. Of 19 responses, all were familiar with the concept of tropes, and 80% of those familiar said that they had visited the TVTropes website. Though opinions were divided as to whether the StoryBuilder interface would fit in with their workflows, 90% of responders said they could see themselves using the system to build stories at some point in the future, even if it would be just for fun.

5   Conclusion

With our approach to interactive narrative generation, we govern the rules of the story domain using an institutional model. This model describes what each agent is permitted and obliged to do at any point in the story. Institutional regimentation of agents acting out a story using story-world norms allows much more flexibility than if the world's rules were strictly enforced. The deontic language of permissions and obligations allows the agents to act out small details of the narrative, while guiding them into an underlying narrative structure.

This narrative structure is composed of story components, described in terms of tropes. Our TropICAL DSL allows for the description of these tropes in a way which can be used to generate deontic logic statements, which are used as input to an ASP solver.

This approach allows the small details to be generated by the character agents, which are not tightly bound by the rules of the story universe, while still giving the author the tools they need with which to structure a dramatic story.

References

1. Baines, V., Padget, J.: A situational awareness approach to intelligent vehicle agents. In: Behrisch, M., Weber, M. (eds.) Modeling Mobility with Open Data. LNM, pp. 77–103. Springer, Cham (2015). https://doi.org/10.1007/978-3-319-15024-6_6
2. Blanco-Vigil, P.C.N.: Agent mediated auctions: the fishmarket metaphor. Ph.D. thesis, Universitat Autònoma de Barcelona (1998)
3. Cliffe, O., De Vos, M., Padget, J.: Specifying and reasoning about multiple institutions. In: Noriega, P., Vázquez-Salceda, J., Boella, G., Boissier, O., Dignum, V., Fornara, N., Matson, E. (eds.) COIN -2006. LNCS (LNAI), vol. 4386, pp. 67–85. Springer, Heidelberg (2007). https://doi.org/10.1007/978-3-540-74459-7_5
4. Lee, J., Li, T., Padget, J.: Towards polite virtual agents using social reasoning techniques. Comput. Animation Virtual Worlds 24(3–4), 335–343 (2013)
5. Lee, S.Y., Mott, B.W., Lester, J.C.: Learning director agent strategies: an inductive framework for modeling director agents. In: Intelligent Narrative Technologies (2011)
6. Lehnert, W.G.: Plot units and narrative summarization. Cogn. Sci. 5(4), 293–331 (1981)
7. Mateas, M., Stern, A.: Façade: An experiment in building a fully-realized interactive drama. In: Game Developers Conference, pp. 4–8 (2003)
8. Propp, V.: Morphology of the Folktale. University of Texas Press, Austin (2010)
9. Robertson, J., Young, R.M.: Modelling character knowledge in plan-based interactive narrative to extend accomodative mediation. In: Ninth Artificial Intelligence and Interactive Digital Entertainment Conference (2013)
10. Rodriguez-Aguilar, J.A., et al.: On the design and construction of Agent-mediated Institutions. Ph.D. thesis, Universidad Autónoma de Barcelona (2001)
11. Short, E.: The Oxford and London Interactive Fiction Meetup (2016). http://www.meetup.com/Oxford-and-London-Interactive-Fiction-Group/events/227889392/. Accessed 19 May 2016
12. Tomaszewski, Z.: On the use of reincorporation in interactive drama. In: Intelligent Narrative Technologies (2011)
13. TV Tropes: TV Tropes an online wiki for media tropes (2016). http://tvtropes.org. Accessed 19 May 2016
14. Vázquez-Salceda, J.: The role of norms and electronic institutions in multi-agent systems applied to complex domains. the harmonia framework. AI Commun. 16(3), 209–212 (2003)

Modular Games AI Benchmark

Benjamin Williams[1]([⊠]), James Jackson[1], Jason Hall[1],
and Christopher J. Headleand[1,2]

[1] Bangor University, Gwynedd, Wales, UK
{bwilliams,cheadleand}@lincoln.ac.uk
[2] University of Lincoln, Lincolnshire, England, UK

Abstract. In this paper we introduce a project developed in Unity 5 which aims to aid in the rapid development and prototyping of games-based experiments. We present the Modular Games Benchmark an openly released tool-kit for games research. Using our framework, experiments can be created quickly without the need for extensive, customised or boilerplate code, aiding in reproducibility and standardisation.

Keywords: Benchmarking · Games AI · Unity 5

1 Introduction

Experimentation involving video games is a common task. Usually for each experiment that is run, initial development is required to first produce the game. As the development of a full game takes a considerable time investment, the test platform is often weak by modern gaming standards. The alternative is to use an existing game which allows customised scripts to be applied, but the underlying game is often a black-box. Alternatively, open-source clones of popular titles have been used, but these come with their own unique issues.

The Modular Games Benchmark is a framework developed in Unity 5 to provide an alternative solution. It is an attempt towards providing a standard toolkit to aid in the rapid development of platforms for games-based experiments. The purpose of the Modular Games Benchmark is to reduce the need for development while fostering the reproducibility of experiments by maintaining a library of common games components and scripts.

2 The Problem

There is a clear disconnect between academic games AI research and commercial products, it has been argued that this is due to a lack of communication [1], but mismatched objectives could also be to blame. The platforms and game styles used in research are often behind those common in industry. For example, while the majority of modern commercial titles are in 3D the majority of games based benchmarking takes place on 2D platforms such as Mario [2–4], Dead-End [5,6] and Pacman [7–10].

© Springer International Publishing AG, part of Springer Nature 2018
P. R. Lewis et al. (Eds.): ALIA 2016, CCIS 732, pp. 138–142, 2018.
https://doi.org/10.1007/978-3-319-90418-4_12

Furthermore, many of these benchmark games are openly released clones of popular titles. Without getting into the complex legalities of cloning a game, there are clear ethical issues which must be considered if we are to promote these unauthorised clones as academic benchmarks. The Modular Games Benchmark is intended as an alternative, including commercial quality game components which can be openly adapted to suit a given experiment. Once experiments are completed, their code can be released back to the benchmark allowing it to be easily reproduced.

3   Modular Games Benchmark

The Modular Games Benchmark has a few key concepts that are used when developing an experiment to be ran using it's framework, which are covered in the documentation. The most fundamental of these concepts are the *primitives* and *instances*.

The *primitive* acts as a template, this includes a list of mutable settings which a given instance can modify. An *instance* is a particular configuration of a given primitive. Each instance of a particular primitive uses the accessible settings for this primitive to create a distinct instance of the given primitive. There are three categories of primitives and instances for usage with the Modular Games Benchmark. A typical experiment ran through the Modular Games Benchmark requires a selection of all three categories of instances in order to create an executable game.

3.1   Environment

An environment primitive determines the world that the game will take place in. Each environment primitive includes a Unity 5 terrain object, and a list of possible settings that can be accessed to alter features (such as the size of the world, or the density of a forest).

The project currently has two environment primitives. The first is a Forest, which can generate forests on a terrain. The second is a maze environment, which can randomly generate a multiconnected environment. Examples of these environments can be seen in Figs. 1a and b.

(a)   (b)

Fig. 1. (a) The forest environment (b) The maze environment

3.2   Characters

Character primitives hold properties for a single class of character (such as a tank). This includes a 'locomotion script' which provides methods used to move and control the character during an experiment. The locomotion script is set of actions available to a given character primitive. These are identical for either the AI, or the player. Furthermore, disparate AI approaches can be tested fairly by providing them with the same set of common navigation controls.

Associated with the character primitive are various other pre-developed modules to enable rapid development. These include a suite of simulated sensors (such as vision) and tools such as weapons (including physics based, and raycast based).

Currently the game includes primitives for 3 types of characters:

- **Capsule:** A very basic character with limited controls. The purpose of this character is to provide a steady base to develop a more complex character upon, and to help understand the basis of what comprises a character primitive.
- **Drone:** A flyable drone character with hovering capabilities.
- **Tank:** A tank character, with a rotatable turret.

This locomotion script implements a common interface, which means it can be used by another script to control the behaviour of a particular character. By using this method of using an interface for defining the functionalities needed to provide locomotion, scripts used to control a particular character can easily be interchanged between different characters in the game.

3.3   Gamemodes

The final category of primitives and instances are gamemodes. Gamemodes outline the interactibility and logic of the experiment. Gamemodes have access to the particular instances that are passed at run-time. For example, gamemodes can spawn teams of characters, keep track of their health, and destroy them when their health is below zero. In this sense then, gamemode instances bring the picked configurations of characters and the environment together, to create a playable game. Without a gamemode instance, an environment would be created but there would be no interaction with it. A gamemode instance is what allows developers access to the chosen characters and environment with which they can develop the basis of their experiments.

The Modular Games Benchmark currently contains two examples of gamemode primitives. The first is a 'Capture the Flag' type of gamemode. The other is a deathmatch scenario, where a number of players are spawned and fight each other until one team wins. Other game modes are currently being developed as part of the ongoing project.

3.4   Parsing

In order to create each game, an XML file reader is used to read in primitives and instances on start up. These are then parsed and used in order to create a menu for the user to choose an experiment with a chosen configuration. Figure 2 illustrates this selection process by the user.

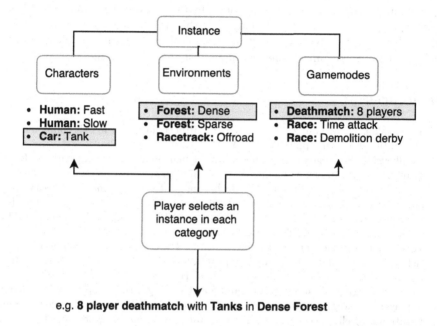

e.g. 8 player deathmatch with **Tanks** in **Dense Forest**

Fig. 2. Players are given and can select a number of instances for each category.

The parsing process makes use of six XML files - two for each Environment, Gamemode and Character. One XML file outlines the possible primitives for each respective category, while the other outlines the mapping of instances to primitives. These are then used to instantiate objects at run-time which represent the chosen instances from each category, which the user can use to develop their experiments.

4   Usage as a Benchmark

The Modular Games Benchmark is intended to be utilised as a benchmark, allowing for user-developed resources to be released back into the project itself. By doing this, researchers conducting future experiments can implementations made by other researchers. Users of the Modular Games Benchmark can make use of this to benchmark their work against previous state of the art developments. Using a rich library of community-developed assets will help ensure that experiments are easier to reproduce while simultaneously increasing the speed of development.

5   Open-Source Release

A number of experiments have recently been conducted using the Modular Games Benchmark. The benchmark has now been openly released on GitHub at http://github.com/blewert/bangor-benchmark/ under a Creative Commons licence to enable free usage. Creating an experiment may require no new development, and simply the creation of new instances using the XML work-flow. However, if new modules are developed within this framework we hope that these will be released back to the project, to both foster reproducibility, and to enable others to benchmark their work against these developments.

References

1. Yannakakis, G.N.: Game AI revisited. In: Proceedings of the 9th conference on Computing Frontiers, pp. 285–292. ACM (2012)
2. Karakovskiy, S., Togelius, J.: The mario AI benchmark and competitions. IEEE Trans. Comput. Intell. AI Games **4**(1), 55–67 (2012)
3. Perez, D., Nicolau, M., O'Neill, M., Brabazon, A.: Evolving behaviour trees for the mario AI competition using grammatical evolution. In: Di Chio, C., et al. (eds.) EvoApplications 2011. LNCS, vol. 6624, pp. 123–132. Springer, Heidelberg (2011). https://doi.org/10.1007/978-3-642-20525-5_13
4. Togelius, J., Karakovskiy, S., Baumgarten, R.: The 2009 mario AI competition. In: IEEE Congress on Evolutionary Computation (CEC) 2010, pp. 1–8. IEEE (2010)
5. He, S., Wang, Y., Xie, F., Meng, J., Chen, H., Luo, S., Liu, Z., Zhu, Q.: Game player strategy pattern recognition and how UCT algorithms apply pre-knowledge of player's strategy to improve opponent AI. In: International Conference on Computational Intelligence for Modelling Control & Automation 2008, pp. 1177–1181. IEEE (2008)
6. Yannakakis, G.N., Levine, J., Hallam, J.: An evolutionary approach for interactive computer games. In: Congress on Evolutionary Computation 2004, CEC2004, vol. 1, pp. 986–993. IEEE (2004)
7. Kalyanpur, A., Simon, M.: Pacman using genetic algorithms and neural networks. University of Maryland (2001)
8. Gallagher, M., Ryan, A.: Learning to play Pac-Man: an evolutionary, rule-based approach. In: The 2003 Congress on Evolutionary Computation 2003, CEC 2003, vol. 4, pp. 2462–2469. IEEE (2003)
9. Szita, I., Lörincz, A.: Learning to play using low-complexity rule-based policies: illustrations through Ms. Pac-Man. J. Artif. Intell. Res. (JAIR) **30**, 659–684 (2007)
10. Galván-López, E., Swafford, J.M., O'Neill, M., Brabazon, A.: Evolving a Ms. Pac-Man controller using grammatical evolution. In: Di Chio, C., et al. (eds.) EvoApplications 2010. LNCS, vol. 6024, pp. 161–170. Springer, Heidelberg (2010). https://doi.org/10.1007/978-3-642-12239-2_17

GCG Aviator: A Decision Support Agent for Career Management

Alina Patelli[1(✉)], Peter R. Lewis[1], Hai Wang[1], Ian Nabney[1], David Bennett[2], and Ralph Lucas[3]

[1] Aston University, Birmingham, UK
{a.patelli,p.lewis,h.wang10,i.t.nabney}@aston.ac.uk
[2] Codevate, Birmingham, UK
david@codevate.com
[3] Good Careers Guide, London, UK
ralph.lucas@goodcareersguide.co.uk

Abstract. Intelligent decision support agents work with heterogeneous information that is constantly changing. They are expected to process that information autonomously and produce results in a form that is easy to understand by a human user. Similarly, online career information is published by different authors in various formats and is subject to continuous editing. Online career advice seekers should be informed by an intuitive, easy to explore view of available career resources. We propose Aviator, a career guidance agent that collates relevant data from different sources, allows viewers to conveniently explore as well as edit that data and provides a means for personalising the users' interaction with the system. We describe, justify and evaluate Aviator's features to highlight their usefulness with providing efficient support for career decisions.

Keywords: Decision support · Ontologies · Autonomic computing

1 Introduction

Making informed decisions about one's career using online resources is a challenging task. Some of the main reasons for that are:

Volume. Online career data forms a large domain of knowledge containing information from various authors (recruiters, education providers, job seekers), in different formats (*lists* of role requirements, course *codes* in JACS[1], comments in *free text*) and published on several websites (recruitment pages, HESA, community forums). It is thus difficult to obtain a global view of the field.

Bias. In most cases, career data repositories (websites, databases, forums) reflect the view of the group (corporations, domain experts, job seekers) that created them. This "author bias" hinders a shared understanding of the field.

---

[1] https://www.hesa.ac.uk/jacs3.

© Springer International Publishing AG, part of Springer Nature 2018
P. R. Lewis et al. (Eds.): ALIA 2016, CCIS 732, pp. 143–147, 2018.
https://doi.org/10.1007/978-3-319-90418-4_13

Abstraction. There is no direct support for managing online career research outputs. Individuals need general purpose tools such as browser bookmarking or spreadsheets to store useful websites or job adds relevant to their career interests. Manually analysing previously gathered career data may be cumbersome.

We propose Aviator, a career guidance agent supporting users in making decisions about their professional lives. Aviator provides:

Perspective. Career knowledge is stored in an ontology and displayed as a navigable graph, where nodes represent various professions and edges illustrate their (hierarchical or sibling-to-sibling) connections. The graph provides users with a visual, global outline of the large **volume** of career data.

Feedforward. Aviator users may annotate online career resources (e.g., website contents) with ontology concepts. Since the annotations are extracted from a common vocabulary, they will be understood in the same way by the entire community, as opposed to the exclusiveness of author **bias**.

Feedback. User experience from exploring and annotating online career resources may be fed back into Aviator by editing the ontology (adding missing concepts, asserting new links, etc.). Allowing the community to curate the common vocabulary eliminates author **bias**.

Customisation. A user's personal collection of annotations is used to generate a *personal ontology*. Organisations also publish personal ontologies, describing, for instance, the profile of an ideal candidate. Comparing the two may reveal the overlap (or lack thereof) between the job seeker's interest and employer's expectations, thus counteracting the **abstraction** effect.

2   Aviator Architecture and Features

Aviator's career knowledge base is stored in a *semantic layer* (an ontology [1] with a reasoner [3]) and managed by an *autonomic manager* [2]. The latter *monitors* requests for viewing or editing nodes, *analyses* the input (verifies the source and collects additional information), *plans* the sequence of actions (run the reasoner to display the requested graph segment, verify ontology consistency after a user edit, etc.) and *executes* them. Aviator supports the following features:

Exploration. To populate the *visualiser* with the first and second order connections of a node, the user inputs the relevant keyword in the *searcher* (Fig. 1). The exploration continues by right-clicking any visible node and selecting Focus. A history tab (not shown in Fig. 1) allows returning to a previous view. Incremental exploration provides the viewer with a **perspective** of the field.

Encapsulation. Several streams of data (job openings, recommended URLs, community discussions) are accessible form the pie menu associated to each node (Fig. 1). This adds to the users' **perspective**.

Tagging. After downloading a browser add-on (top dashboard menu), users may annotate webpages with concepts from the ontology (Fig. 2). This way, explorers increase their careers' knowledge as well as **feed it forward** to other users.

Editing. Concepts and properties can be added/deleted to/from the ontology, thus **feeding** community knowledge **back** into Aviator. Figure 4 shows a new child node being added to APPLIED BIOLOGICAL SCIENCES.

Customisation. Explorers may view the segment of the ontology that is relevant to them (via `Personal explore` in the dashboard) showing all concepts used as tags by the current user (`Me` in Fig. 3) along with their first order connections.

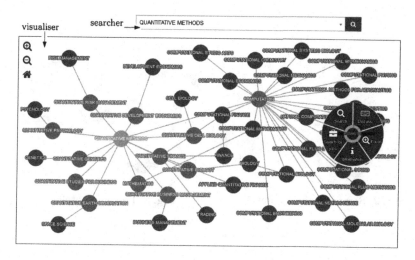

Fig. 1. Ontology exploration

3   Evaluation

Encapsulation. (accessing several relevant streams of information via a node's pie menu) and **tagging** online career resources with annotations extracted from the ontology can be experienced by logging into Aviator[2] (user name `johnsmith`, password `gcgtesting`). Incremental **exploration** and **customisation** are underpinned by DL queries, with the execution times in Table 1 (ultimately showing how long it takes to expand a node in the visualiser,

Table 1. Ontology operations duration (DigitalOcean: 4 CPUs @ 8 GB RAM)

Node links	Query runtime [ms]
<50	132
50 – 100	532
>100	1231

---

[2] https://gcg-test.codevate.com/login.

given the node's connectivity). **Editing** relies on classification (ontology consistency verification). The FaCT++ reasoner [3] takes ~91 s to classify an ontology with 15000 concepts where 5% of the nodes have 50 first and second order connections or less, 75% have between 50 and 100 neighbours and the rest have over 100 connections.

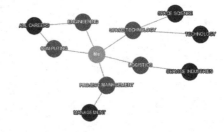

Fig. 2. Semantic annotations   **Fig. 3.** Personal ontology

Fig. 4. Ontology editing

4   Conclusions

Aviator enables the incremental **exploration** of the knowledge graph underpinning the career domain. Various types of relevant information (jobs, user reviews, etc.) are **encapsulated** in each node of the graph and are easily accessible. The career knowledge stored and curated by Aviator can be used to **tag** new online resources discovered by users, as well as **edited** to reflect the point of view of the wider community. Finally, Aviator users can **customise** their experience by generating a personal ontology, capturing their professional profiles and interests.

These features are enabled by a *semantic layer* and self-managed by an *autonomic control loop*, a hybrid approach that, given our results, is successful at providing intelligent decision support in the field of careers.

References

1. Baader, F., Calvanese, D., McGuiness, D., Nardi, D., Patel-Schneider, P. (eds.): The Description Logic Handbook: Theory Implementation and Applications. Cambridge University Press, Cambridge (2003)
2. Kephart, J., Chess, D.: The vision of autonomic computing. Computer **36**(1), 41–50 (2003)
3. Tsarkov, D., Horrocks, I.: FaCT++ description logic reasoner: system description. In: Furbach, U., Shankar, N. (eds.) IJCAR 2006. LNCS (LNAI), vol. 4130, pp. 292–297. Springer, Heidelberg (2006). https://doi.org/10.1007/11814771_26

Author Index

Printed in the United States
By Bookmasters